THE
LITTLE
BOOK
OF
GALWAY

HELEN LEE

The
History
Press

First published 2018
This paperback edition published 2020

The History Press
97 St George's Place, Cheltenham,
Gloucestershire, GL50 3QB
www.thehistorypress.co.uk

British Library Cataloguing in Publication Data.
A catalogue record for this book is available from the British Library.

ISBN 978 0 7509 9461 3
Typesetting and origination by The History Press
Printed and bound in Great Britain by TJ Books Limited

CONTENTS

Co Mayo

Co Roscommon

Leenane

Lough MASK

Clifden

Lough Corrib

Co
GALWAY

Tuam

Oughterard

Mountbellew

Galway

Athenry

Ballinasloe

Oranmore

Inis Mor

Loughrea

Inis Maan

Inisheer

Portumna

Kinvara

Gort

LOUGH DERG

Co Clare

Co Tipperary

1

THE HISTORY OF
GALWAY: A TIMELINE

Over the course of 10,000 years of history, from the arrival of the first people in about 8,000 BC, Ireland has had her share of invasions and oppression, wars and battles, famine and strife, progress and prosperity. Throughout this history Galway and her people have played their part.

As past generations tried to explain the origins of our race, they created tales of mythical tribes such as the Fir Bolg and the Tuatha De Dannan. Legend holds that these two had a battle in Connacht, on the shores of Lough Corrib. The defeated Fir Bolg went to the Aran Islands to lick their wounds.

The Celts and their influences arrived around 500 BC. Their lasting legacy to Ireland is the Irish language. The largest Irish-speaking area or 'Gaeltacht' in Ireland today is in Co. Galway, taking in most of Connemara and the Aran Islands.

Although there is no reference to St Patrick in Galway, perched on top of Croagh Patrick in neighbouring Co. Mayo he would have seen the distant mountains of Connemara, with its lakes and bogs. Other saints followed him and settled in remote parts of Galway, such as the Aran Islands.

The Vikings concentrated their attacks on the eastern side of Ireland. However, in 807AD they turned their attentions to the western seaboard, attacking the monastery at Roscam; but for reasons best known to themselves they did not establish any settlements in the west. Perhaps they found the tribes of the wild countryside too fierce even for them?

In the thirteenth century, the Anglo-Normans led by Richard de Burgo were the first outsiders to make a settlement in Galway.

They chose a spot where the fast-flowing River Gaillimh enters the sea. This settlement would become the city of Galway.

By the fifteenth century, fourteen merchant families, including the Lynches and the Martins, built trade links with England, France and Spain. In 1484 they were granted a city charter, which allowed them to elect a mayor and pass laws. Oliver Cromwell's soldiers called these merchant families 'the Tribes of Galway'. His arrival brought turmoil to Ireland and particularly to the west. His decision to banish Catholic landowners to 'Hell or to Connacht' suggests that the region was seen as a wild, untamed outpost, not worthy of settlement by the Protestant classes. Among the Catholics to lose lands in the Cromwellian period were the prosperous merchant families of Galway city. Their losses were to be the gain of families such as the Eyres and the Meyricks. The latter part of the seventeenth century brought further turmoil.

In the 1680s the Glorious Revolution saw the throne of England taken over by the Protestant King William of Orange. While no battles were fought in England, the war between William and his deposed father-in-law James II spilled over into Ireland. The bloodiest battle was fought at Aughrim, outside Ballinasloe in 1691. The defeat of the Catholic King James led to the Flight of the Wild Geese, members of the Tribes of Galway among them, and the implementation of the Penal Laws in Ireland. This led to further changes in land ownership, and the merchant tribes finally losing their grip on Galway. Some, however, had converted to Protestantism in order to hold on to their lands.

By the eighteenth century, the Protestant Ascendancy was the ruling class. Those families who had supported King William were rewarded with estates. The Martins built Ballynahinch Castle, the Dillons built Clonbrock and the D'Arcys built Clifden Castle and Killtullagh House. Meanwhile the impoverished Catholics rented plots of land on these estates and scratched out a living, feeding themselves on potatoes.

The failure of the potato crops in 1845 and 1846 brought devastation, particularly to the west of Ireland. The tenant farmers depended on that crop for sustenance and with no food and harsh weather, they were rendered destitute. Landowners evicted tenants who had no money to pay rents.

In Co. Galway some of the landlords bankrupted themselves in an effort to help their starving tenants. Others did little to help.

By the end of the nineteenth century, some prosperity had returned to Galway city with the opening of mills along the banks of the renamed River Corrib and the opening of a university. Rural Galway faced further turmoil as the Land War saw the conflict of land distribution come to a head.

Galway played its part in the struggle for Irish independence. In the early twentieth century, the Irish Volunteers of County Galway, like their Dublin colleagues rebelled at the Easter of 1916.

Throughout the twentieth century, Galway evolved into a modern, busy city, while retaining some of its medieval features. Connemara's lack of development in past centuries has meant that the unspoilt beauty of the region is now its biggest asset. Tourism now suppliments farming as the economy of rural Co. Galway.

The following is a timeline of the history that made Galway:

3000 BC: Middens, the rubbish tips of our ancestors, found in locations around the Galway coast, indicate that early settlers in Galway were partial to oysters, which are celebrated in the county to this day.

3300 BC: A 'bog body', found in 1929, in a bog at Stoney Island on the Co. Galway shores of Lough Derg are the oldest preserved human remains found in Ireland.

2500 BC: A log boat dating from this period was found at the bottom of Lough Derg as recently as 2014.

1100 BC: Although difficult to date, it is thought that the semi-circular fort of Dun Aengus, perched on a cliff edge on the largest of the Aran Islands, Inishmore, was built at this time.

500 BC: The Iron Age brought the Gaelic Celts to Ireland.

400–200 BC: Gallagh Man, a Celt, was murdered by strangulation. He was covered by his deerskin cape and buried in a bog near what is now Castleblakeney. When the O'Kelly family discovered him in 1821, instead of alerting the authorities, they began to charge people to see their historic find. The Royal Irish Academy took him for preservation in 1829 and he is now at the National Museum of Ireland.

100 BC: The Gaelic language is spoken throughout Ireland, which is divided into Celtic kingdoms. The westernmost kingdom is Connacht.

100 BC–AD 100: At Turoe, near Loughrea, can be found one of the best examples of Celtic artwork in Ireland. The Turoe Stone is a granite stone which stands about 1m (3ft) in height. While the base has no decoration, a series of step-like carvings circle the middle. However, it is the domed top of the sculpture which has the most significant carvings. Decorated with relief carvings of swirls, lozenges and trumpet shapes, possibly inspired by foliage and animals, the Turoe Stone is a fine example of Celtic La Tène artwork. This style of European Iron Age art takes its name from the Swiss village where a hoard of items with similar art work to that on the Turoe Stone was discovered in the nineteenth century. The Turoe Stone was originally located at the Rath of Feerwore, but was moved in the nineteenth century to its current location outside Turoe House for use as a garden ornament. Because of its phallic shape, it has been suggested that the Turoe Stone may originally have been a symbol of fertility, and the focal point of some Celtic ritual at the Rath.

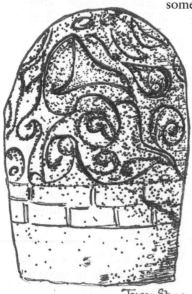

Turoe Stone

484: St Enda builds a monastery on the Aran Islands.

c. 500: It is possible that there is already a settlement on the west side of the River Gaillimh(later the Corrib) where fishing is the main occupation. This area is later known as the Claddagh.

540: While travelling in search of a site for a church, a wheel on St Jarlath's charriot breaks, east of Lough Corrib. He decides that he will build his church on that spot. The site is Tuam.

577: St Brendan the Navigator dies at Annaghdown, site of a monastery that he founded. He is buried at Clonfert, another of his monasteries.

c. **600:** St Colman mac Duagh is buried at his monastery at Kilmacdugh.

795: The Vikings come to the west and attack the island of Inishbofin.

807: The Vikings come back and this time they target the monasteries. They attack the monastic settlement at Roscam on Galway Bay.

1111: The diocesan system introduced to administer the Church in Ireland is set up at the Synod of Rath Breasail. This establishes the dioceses of Clonfert and Tuam.

1124: Turlough O'Connor (1088–1156), King of Connacht, realises that the mouth of the River Gaillimh is the most vulnerable point of his territories. He builds a castle, Bun Gaillimhe. This is the beginning of the settlement that will become 'Galway'.

1152: Another Synod is held which reorganises the Church. At the prompting of Turlough O'Connor, Tuam becomes an archdiocese.

1156: Turlough O'Connor, the High King of Ireland and King of Connacht, dies.

1166: Rory O'Connor (1116–1198), son of Turlough, becomes High King. He will be the last High King of Ireland.

1175: Rory O'Connor recognises the English King Henry II, now Lord of Ireland, as his overlord. In return he is recognised as the high king of territories not held by Anglo-Norman barons. This applies to most of Connacht, as the Anglo-Normans have not yet ventured west of the Shannon.

1226: King Henry III grants the kingdom of Connacht to Richard de Burgo (1194–1242), 1st Lord of Connacht.

1230: Richard de Burgo comes west of the Shannon to claim his territories.

1232: Richard de Burgo builds a castle at the mouth of the River Gaillimh, where O'Connor's fort had stood a century earlier. The O'Connors and O'Flahertys are not pleased to see him. They burn his castle to the ground and de Burgo has to retreat.

1235: The Anglo-Normans return to Connacht in force and defeat Felim O'Connor. Richard de Burgo is aided by the de Bermighams, the de Lacys and the Fitzgeralds.

1236: The town of Loughrea is founded by Richard de Burgo.

1238: Meiler de Bermingham, 2nd Baron of Athenry, builds Athenry Castle and a Dominican friary.

1247: The O'Connors attack the town of Galway. A report of the attack is the first recorded mention of Galway as a town.

1252: The first Franciscan friary in Connacht is built at Claregalway by the Anglo-Norman John de Cogan, who came west with Richard de Burgo.

1270: Walter de Burgo (*c.* 1230–1271), 1st Earl of Ulster (created 1265) and Lord of Connacht, begins to build walls around the settlement of Galway. He pays for the defensive structure by taxing goods that are brought into the town.

1271: Walter's son, Richard de Burgo (1259–1326), becomes 2nd Earl of Ulster and Lord of Connacht. He becomes known as 'The Red Earl'. Work begins on the Red Earl's Hall in the town of Galway. It replaces an earlier castle and is the largest stone building in the town.

1296: The Franciscans arrive and build a friary in the town of Galway.

1300: The Carmelite abbey at Loughrea is built on the orders of Richard de Burgo, the Red Earl.

1312: Galway's town walls are reinforced to protect it from further attacks by the Gaelic clans and particularly the O'Flahertys.

1315: Rory and Felim O'Connor are at war over the kingship of Connacht. Felim wins out and aligns himself with Edward Bruce, who has been sent to Ireland by his brother King Robert I of Scotland to convince the Gaelic chieftains of Ireland to ally themselves with Scotland in an attempt to overthrow the English.

1316: Felim O'Connor, the King of Connacht, goes to war with the Anglo-Normans. He is killed at the Battle of Athenry.

1320: St Nicholas's Church is built in Galway by the Anglo-Norman Lynch family.

1333: William de Burgo, Lord of Connacht and 3rd Earl of Ulster, known as 'the Brown Earl', is murdered.

His death leads to a power struggle in the de Burgo family. His only child, Elizabeth, flees to England and marries Lionel, Duke of Clarence. King Edward IV will be a direct descendant. This leaves her two cousins, Edmund and William, to divide the de Burgo territories between them. They renounce their allegiance to the Crown, adopt Irish ways and their name becomes Burke. They are one of the Anglo-Norman families to 'become more Irish than the Irish themselves'. Edmund becomes Eamonn na Féasoige or Eamonn of the Beard and head of what will become the Lower McWilliams or MacWilliam Burke clan, taking control of the western and northern territories of Connacht. William becomes Ulick an Fhíona or Ulick of the Wine and heads up what becomes the Upper McWilliams or Clanricarde Burke clan, taking control of the town of Galway and the east and south of Connacht.

1375: Through the efforts of a growing number of merchant families, the town of Galway is allowed the right to hold markets for the sale of animal hides and wool. Galway is now recognised as a town just like Cork, Dublin and Waterford. However, the Mac William Burkes are lords of the town and are not royalists. Edward III revokes the charter and Galway does not get official recognition as a town again until 1395.

1380: Galway is the main point of entry for wine imported into Ireland.

1395: King Richard II raises Galway to the status of Royal Borough. This allows the town's people to elect an official called the Sovereign, who up until now was appointed by the Burke lords. This effectively brings their power to an end. The city is now loyal to the Crown.

1400: By the beginning of the fifteenth century, Galway is a thriving port town with its own church, civic building and a defensive wall. It has trade links with Spain, Portugal and France developed through the efforts of fourteen families, mostly of Anglo-Norman descent. The 'Tribes of Galway', as they later become known, are the Athys, Blakes, Bodkins, Brownes, D'Arcys, Deans, Frenchs, Fonts, Joyces, Kirwans, Lynches, Martins, Morrises and Skerritts. Exports of wool and linen, sheepskins and leather, horses and cattle, tallow and fish are traded for minerals such as coal and iron and luxuries such as wines, spices and silks.

1412: The town of Galway is burnt to the ground. It is not clear if this is as a result of an attack from the Mac Williams or whether a thatch-and-wood structure caught fire, but this is the first of many fires that Galway will experience over the next century.

1442: The first stone bridge spanning the river at Galway is built, linking the town with the west.

1460: The first by-laws governing Galway are passed. They exclude the Gaelic Irish from inside the town walls.

1477: Christopher Columbus visits Galway. He probably prays at St Nicholas's Church, which is dedicated to the patron saint of sailors. He may also have been in search of information about St Brendan the Navigator's legendary voyage across the Atlantic in the sixth century.

1484: Richard III grants Galway a City Charter. The people can now elect a Mayor and set up a Corporation to govern the city.

1485: St Nicholas's Church becomes a collegiate church, by Papal Bull from Pope Innocent VIII. This takes the church out of the control of the Archbishop of Tuam and means that it can be administered by a warden and eight vicars appointed by the City Corporation.

1486: Pyerse Lynch becomes the first Mayor of Galway, the first in a long line of Lynches who will hold the post. Galway Corporation has the power to pass statutes.

1492: Mayor James Lynch Fitzstephen hangs his own son for murder.

1500: Another fire destroys the city. This gives the merchant families the opportunity to build themselves new stone 'castles'. Blakes's Castle and Lynch's Castle date from this period.

1504: The Battle of Knockdoe.

1518: Galway Corporation is now passing statutes. A statute is passed which bans the Burkes and the MacWilliams and any family whose name begins with 'Mac' or 'Ó' from the streets of Galway.

1522: A statute declares that any man wishing to be elected a freeman of the city of Galway must 'speak the English tongue and shave his upper lip weekly'.

1526: A statute licensing the manufacture and sale of alcohol is passed by Galway Corporation.

1527: The game of hurling is banned from inside the city walls. It is unlikely that this is for health and safety reasons, but rather that the game was seen as a Gaelic pastime and not something that a self-respecting town's man should play.

1538: The Franciscan monks at Ross Errily Abbey oppose King Henry VIII's Dissolution of the Monasteries. Two hundred monks are imprisoned. They later return to the abbey.

1543: On 1 July Ulick Burke, head of the Upper McWilliam family, is created 1st Earl of Clanricarde and Baron of Dunkellin under King Henry VIII's 'Surrender and Regrant' policy. He is loyal to the Crown and has 'gone over'.

1550: King Edward VI sanctions the transfer of St Nicholas Collegiate Church to Protestantism.

1576: Sir Henry Sidney, Queen Elizabeth I's Lord Deputy of Ireland, creates the modern county of Galway, defining the borders between it and the neighbouring counties of Mayo, Roscommon and Clare.

1584: The Spanish Arch is built as an extension of the city walls.

1588: The King of Spain's failed attempt to invade England ends with his armada fleeing the English navy via the North Sea, around the north coast of Scotland and down the west coast of Ireland. One ship, the *Falon Blanco Mediano*, sinks off the coast at Barna. Seventy Spaniards make it to the shore, only to be rounded up and executed.

1597: Red Hugh O'Donnell, during his campaign against English rule in Ireland, burns the town of Athenry. The castle and the abbey survive the onslaught. He then heads to Galway, where the city leaders reprimand him for turning against the Crown. He burns part of the city outside the walls and then goes on his way. He eventually flees Ireland after he is defeated by Elizabethan forces at the Battle of Kinsale, 1601.

1618: Portumna Castle, a fortified manor house, is built by the 4th Earl of Clanricarde.

1630: A square plot outside the East Gate of the city is dedicated for public amusement. This later becomes Eyre Square.

1649: King Charles I is beheaded in London. The king's son, the future Charles II, writes to Galway Corporation thanking them for their loyalty. It is possible that the axe man came from Galway.

1649: The plague hits Galway.

1652: In April, Galway surrenders to Sir Charles Coote, a general in Oliver Cromwell's army, after a nine-month siege of the city. The Cromwellian soldiers are the first to use the term 'the Tribes of Galway'. They are not being complementary.

1652: The Act of Settlement formalises the transplantation of Irish Catholics to Connacht after Cromwell famously tells them they can go 'to Hell or to Connacht'. Some estate owners convert to Protestantism to avoid having their lands confiscated. Those banished to Connacht are given small estates of poor land. Soldiers who fought for Cromwell are rewarded with land throughout Ireland. John Eyre is given lands in East Galway, where he calls his estate Eyrecourt.

1654: Catholics are prohibited from holding office on Galway Corporation.

1686: James Kirwan becomes Mayor of Galway. He is the first Catholic to hold the post in twenty-five years.

1691: The Battle of Aughrim.

1717: The Penal Laws were enforced after the War of the Two Kings, punishing Catholics who had supported King James II. Despite these oppressive laws, the people of Galway acclaimed Queen Anne when she came to the throne on the death of her brother-in-law, William III. This obedience did not spare them from the harsh laws that were being implemented by 1703. Laws were passed which prevented Catholics from buying property within the city walls. Another put a 4 o'clock curfew on trade for Catholics. Gradually Catholics were forced from public office and the main officials of Galway Corporation were soon Protestant. Some of the rising Protestants felt sympathy for the ousted Catholics and pleaded for a softening of the Penal Laws, while other officials wanted full implementation. In 1717 two aldermen, Thomas Simcoles and Edward Barratt, petitioned Parliament in London, saying that Galway was a haven for 'Popish' nuns, priests and friars, and that the laws in Galway were too lenient towards Catholics. The Jacobites had not gone away. The Old Pretender, the son of King James II, had attempted a rising in Scotland in 1715 in an effort to once again place a Catholic king on the throne. A bill, 'for the better regulating of Galway and for strengthening the Protestant interest therein', was passed by both the House of Commons and the House of Lords in December 1717. This became known as 'The Galway Act'.

1730: The Catholic 'Tribes of Galway' are no longer involved in trade and in their reduced circumstances some turn to smuggling to make a living.

1793: The Connaught Rangers Regiment of the British Army is established.

1812: John Darcy begins to build Clifden Castle on his Connemara estate.

1824: Richard Martin, MP for Galway and owner of Ballynahinch Castle, founds the Royal Society for the Prevention of Cruelty to Animals.

1831: In the wake of the 1829 Catholic Emancipation Act, which repealed the Penal Laws, the Catholic Diocese of Galway is created. The Catholic parish church of St Nicholas becomes the pro-cathedral for the new diocese.

1839: Twelve coastguards at Roundstone, Connemara are drowned on 6 January, the Night of the Big Wind.

1841: Daniel O'Connell addresses a crowd in Eyre Square on the subject of repealing the 1801 Act of Union.

1841: The combined population of Galway city and county reaches approximately 440,000.

1842: A gallery at St Nicholas's Catholic Pro-Cathedral collapses during the 6 a.m. Christmas Morning Mass, killing thirty-seven.

1847: Sir William Henry Gregory was MP for Dublin in 1847, the year in which he inherited the family estate of Coole Park, Gort. This year was also known as 'Black '47'. The potato crop on which the tenant farmers of Ireland depended for food, had failed two years in a row. The tenant farmers were starving, and facing a harsh winter. A Poor Relief Bill was going through the Houses of Parliament to address the plight of the Irish people. The bill would put the responsibility of providing poor relief on the ratepayers and landowners. Sir Gregory proposed a clause which stated that 'no tenant holding more than a quarter acre of land should be eligible for public assistance either in the workhouse or outside it.' The 'Gregory Clause' was included in the bill.

However, since many tenants who held leases on land over a quarter acre were also in dire need of assistance, they had to surrender all claim to their land before they could get relief. This was a form of eviction in reverse, with the tenant deciding to leave his land, as opposed to being evicted. Landlords abused this loophole, clearing the land of tenants.

1847: The Galway Workhouse was built to accommodate 800 destitute people. In 1847 it was home to 3,000.

1847: Some landlords tried to help their tenants, such as the Martins of Ballynahinch and Lord Gort of Lough Cutra.

1848: Queen's College Galway opens its doors to sixty-three students.

1848: It is estimated that 3,000 beggars are roaming the streets of Galway.

1849: 20,588 deaths are recorded due to famine in Co. Galway.

1849: A ship, the *St John*, leaves Galway, bound for Boston, in September carrying passengers from many parts of Galway and Co. Clare. On 7 October she is wrecked on rocks in Massachusetts Bay, with great loss of life.

1851: Lord Gort of the Lough Cutra sells his estate – he has bankrupted himself during the Famine, as he did not force his tenants to pay their rents.

1851: The combined population of Galway city and county has dropped to approximately 322,000, reduced by 120,000 from 1841. The Famine has taken a huge toll on the population of Galway.

1851: Galway and Dublin are finally connected by train. The journey time is four hours.

1867: Kylemore Abbey is built in Connemara by Mitchell Henry of Manchester.

1882: The Maamtrasna Murders.

1886: Charles Stewart Parnell addresses a crowd in Eyre Square on the subject of Home Rule.

1886: The impact of the Land War reaches Galway. An eviction from the Clanricarde Estate leads to a riot near Woodford.

1895: The railway connects Galway with Clifden.

1905: St Brendan's Catholic Cathedral, for the diocese of Clonfert, is consecrated in Loughrea.

1907: Marconi opens a transatlantic wireless station near Clifden, connecting with Glace Bay in Canada.

1911: Jim Larkin, the founder of the trade union movement in Ireland, addresses a crowd in Eyre Square.

1917: The Galway National Shell Factory begins producing '18-Pounder' shells for the war effort. One thousand shells are produced a week by 115 employees, mostly women, until the end of the First World War.

1919: Alcock and Brown complete the first transatlantic flight. They crash land in a bog near Clifden.

1916: The Easter Rising of 1916 sees almost 1,000 Irish Volunteers rebel in Co. Galway.

1920: Galway does not escape the War of Independence; it sees a number of atrocities, including the kidnap and murder of Fr Michael Griffin.

1930: The last cottage of the Claddagh Village is pulled down.

1941: Coole Park House, the seat of the Celtic Literary Revival, is demolished.

1954: The first Galway Oyster Festival takes place.

1960: The Tynagh Mines near Loughrea are opened and the mining of lead and zinc begins.

1965: Galway's new Roman Catholic Cathedral is consecrated and dedicated to St Nicholas of Myra and our Lady Assumed into Heaven.

1975: The last railway branch line in Galway, linking Loughrea to Attymon on the main Galway–Dublin line, is closed.

1979: Pope John Paul II visits Galway.

1984: Galway city commemorates 500 years as a city.

2009: The new M6 motorway linking Galway and Dublin is completed.

2012: The Volvo Round the World Yacht Race finishes in Galway.

2020: Galway is the European City of Culture.

2

THE CITY OF GALWAY

The Vikings brought the concept of building towns to Ireland, but they did not establish a settlement in Connacht. They plundered and pillaged, but did not stay. Had they decided to settle, the ideal place would have been on the banks of the River Gaillimh, which took its name from the daughter of the mythical King Bressal. Galvia, or Gaillimh, fell into the fast-flowing waters, never to be seen again. In the nineteenth century, the river officially became the Corrib, taking its name from the lake which it drains.

In 1124, Turlough O'Connor, the King of Connacht, reinforced the original settlement of Baile an Srúthan ('the Town of Streams') at the mouth of the river, calling it Bun Gaillimhe. His kingdom of Connacht was bordered by water on both sides: the Atlantic to the west and Lough Corrib to the east. But the mouth of the river was vulnerable to attack. Over a century later, this is where the Irish and the Anglo-Normans came to blows.

The first Anglo-Normans came to Ireland in 1170. It would be another sixty years before their influence spread west of the Shannon. Richard de Burgo arrived at Bun Gaillimhe in 1232. He built a castle. The native Irish soon destroyed this, beginning centuries of friction between them and the invaders. Richard returned in 1235, better prepared for opposition. He had a bigger army and built a sturdier settlement, which would later become the city of Galway.

THE WALLS OF GALWAY

By 1270 Walter de Burgo, Richard's son, was building a defensive wall around the settlement. He levied taxes on goods coming into the town to pay for this massive and necessary defensive structure. By the 1400s the walls enclosed an area of 11 hectares (27 acres), making it a smaller town than nearby Athenry. The main gates to the town were on the eastern, western and northern sides. The East Gate was flanked by defensive towers and overlooked a flat green area, which today is Eyre Square. Entering Galway through this gate led to the main street. Today Shop Street, leading onto Quay Street, follows the route to Galway's medieval harbour. The street passing by St Nicholas's Collegiate Church led to the West Gate and the only bridge spanning the river in medieval times. In addition to the gates there were thirteen towers of varying sizes around the wall, although none of them were on the west side, the river being defence enough.

In 1442, a lookout tower was completed at the West Gate. An inscription on the gate read 'From the ferocious O'Flahertys, Good Lord deliver us'. After 200 years of settlement the Normans had not integrated with the Gaelic families. They even had a law which excluded people whose names began with 'Mac' or 'Ó" from within the town walls.

The walls of the city were reinforced in the 1690s in anticipation of an attack during the War of the Two Kings. Galway had sided with the Catholic King James II. The expected siege of Galway began on 19 July 1691, following the Williamite victory at the Battle of Aughrim. The people of Galway surrendered three days later, knowing that their walls could not withstand a bombardment of Williamite cannon fire. This was the last time the city needed defensive walls. During the eighteenth century they began to crumble and disappear, making way for new buildings as the city began to sprawl beyond its medieval confines. Today, remnants of the walls are preserved. The best example is the restored Shoemaker Tower, which was once the corner where the east and south sides of the city's medieval walls met. Today it is tastefully incorporated into the Eyre Square Shopping Centre.

THE SPANISH ARCH

One of Galway city's most iconic features is the Spanish Arch. Located by the banks of the gushing Corrib, it was built in 1584 as an extension of the city wall. Originally it comprised four arches, providing shelter for ships docked in the medieval quay. In later years this area was reclaimed from the river, and became the Fish Market.

When first built, the arch was known in Irish as 'Ceann Balla' or 'Head of the Wall'. It became known as 'An Poirse Caoch' or 'the Blind Arch' when one of the arches was blocked up. The current name is a nostalgic reminder of a time when Galway had strong commercial links with Spain.

On 1 November 1755 an earthquake erupted in the Atlantic Ocean off the coast of Portugal. The tsunami which followed the Lisbon earthquake washed away large parts of that city, killing nearly 40,000 people. The effects of the tsunami were felt along the Irish coastline. In Galway the impact caused damage to the Spanish Arch.

THE RED EARL'S HALL

Richard de Burgo (1259–1326), 2nd Earl of Ulster, Lord of Connacht and grandson of the founder of Galway, was known as the 'Red Earl'. In 1271 he replaced an earlier castle with a larger stone building from which he administered the town. The Red Earl's Hall, as it became known, was a long room lined with pillars which supported the high roof. The walls were buttressed on the outside. It was the largest and most important building in thirteenth-century Galway.

In 1395 King Richard II granted Galway borough status. In addition to recognising Galway as an official town, this grant also allowed the town's people to elect a Sovereign, an early incarnation of a Mayor. This weakened the de Burgos' grip on the affairs of Galway. Throughout the fifteenth century, a group of fourteen families came to prominence. Recognising the benefits of their coastal location, they developed trade links with Bristol, London, Bordeaux, Seville and Lisbon. They brought prosperity to the town and would later be known as 'the Tribes of Galway'.

The decline of the de Burgos was matched by the decay of the Red Earl's Hall. In a detailed map of Galway from 1651, the Hall is depicted as a ruin. In 1820, James Hardiman published a history of Galway in which he remarked that there was no longer any trace of the Red Earl's Hall. But its history does not end there. In 1997 plans were drawn up to extend the city's Custom House. The excavations for the new foundations revealed the site of the Red Earl's Hall. Archaeologists moved on to the site, at Druid's Lane. The plans for the Custom House were changed and today the public can see the remains of Richard de Burgo's castle from a viewing platform.

ST NICHOLAS' COLLEGIATE CHURCH

In 1320 a stone church was built within the town walls of Galway. It was dedicated to St Nicholas of Myra, the patron saint of sailors and thieves. It can be assumed that his patronage was sought for the sailors coming and going from the fledgling port and not for the thieves. He is also the patron saint of children and better known today as Santa Claus.

The extension of the church in the fifteenth century is an indication of the prosperity of Galway at that time. The Lynches and Frenches funded the building of two new aisles on either side of the original nave, which gave the church its unusual three-gabled west façade. This is how it would have appeared when Christopher Columbus came and prayed here in 1477. Perhaps he had heard of the exploits of St Brendan the Navigator, who allegedly crossed the Atlantic in the sixth century. The intrepid saint's story may have sown the seeds of an idea in Columbus's head. Fifteen years later he crossed the Atlantic himself.

The interior of St Nicholas has all the hallmarks of a medieval church: a sixteenth-century baptismal font that is still in use, an apprentice's pillar, a knight's tomb. The benefactors of the church are also well represented with the Lynch window tomb, which bears their coat of arms, and the Lynch altar tomb in the 'flamboyant' style, all in the south transept. Many of the carvings on these tombs are defaced, a legacy of the Cromwellian soldiers who, in addition to vandalising the church, also stabled their horses in it.

St Nicholas' Church was originally a Catholic parish church in the diocese of Tuam. When Galway was granted city status in 1484, the governors of the new city appealed to Pope Innocent VIII for control of their own church. He designated St Nicholas' a collegiate church, giving the newly established City Corporation the power to appoint a Warden and eight vicars to administer the church.

During the reign of King Edward VI the church was taken over by the Protestant community. It reverted briefly to Catholicism before Cromwell arrived, and again during the Williamite and Jacobite war of the 1690s. Since then St Nicholas' has been a place of worship for the Anglican parishioners of Galway. However, Catholic services were once again held there in 2005. The nearby St Augustine's Catholic church was closed for refurbishment and while the work was ongoing, the Protestant clergy accommodated the Catholic congregation at St Nicholas', even changing their Sunday Service time to fit the temporary arrangement.

Inside the church, the walls are covered in memorial plaques. High on the south wall is a memorial plaque to Jane Eyre, a real-life eighteenth-century figure and not Charlotte Brontë's fictional governess. Jane was married to Edward Eyre, who granted Eyre Square to the city.

Originally the church had a simple tower, the top of which was replaced by a spire in the 1680s. The tower parapets were restored to the base of the spire in 1883 and in 1898 a clock mechanism was installed in the tower. However, it would only support three clocks, on the east, west and south sides. The north face of the spire faces towards the Poor Clare Convent, leading Catholics in the city to suggest that the Protestant clergy would not give the good nuns 'the time of day'.

St Nicholas' Collegiate Church is the oldest parish church in continuous use in Ireland.

THE TRIBES OF GALWAY

One would be forgiven for thinking that Galway got its nickname 'City of the Tribes' from the wild, unruly Gaelic families who ruled over Connemara for centuries. But the famous 'Tribes of Galway' were the fourteen gentrified merchant families who made Galway a thriving trading seaport in the 1400s.

Having wrestled control of the city from the founding de Burgos, they recognised the advantage of their maritime location. The Athy, Blake, Browne, Bodkin, D'Arcy, Deane, French, Font, Joyce, Kirwan, Lynch, Martin, Morris and Skerritt families built a harbour and established trade links with Bristol, London, Orkney, Amsterdam, Saint-Malo, Nantes, La Rochelle, Bordeaux, Lisbon and Seville.

They exported animal hides, wool, cloth, tallow and salted fish, and imported iron and salt, but also luxuries such as wine, spices and silks. By the sixteenth century they were trading with the Gaelic lords outside the walls, buying turf and sheep from Connemara. The pinnacle of these merchant families' achievements came when King Richard III granted Galway a city charter in 1484.

The lineage and genealogy of the 'Tribes of Galway' reveal the extent to which they intermarried. Take as an example Sir Thomas Blake, who lived in Galway in the seventeenth century. He was the 4th Baronet Blake of Galway. He married three times, and each wife was a member of another tribe family. The first was Mary Martin, the second was Elinor Lynch and the third wife was Mary French of the Monivea Frenchs.

It was Oliver Cromwell who brought about the decline of the 'Tribes of Galway'. His soldiers referred to them as 'the Tribes', in a derogatory sense. Their lands were confiscated and redistributed to newly arrived Protestant families, such as the Eyres. Some, such as Sir Thomas Blake, converted to Protestantism in 1652 to prevent the family estate being confiscated.

After the Battle of Aughrim, in 1691 those of the Tribes who refused to convert to Protestantism felt the full force of the Penal Laws. They were not allowed to trade or hold positions of power. Many fled with the Wild Geese, and others turned their hand to smuggling goods on their established trade routes.

Athy

The Athys have French ancestry. Gerard de Athy served King Richard I in France. Both he and his son are mentioned in Magna Carta of 1215. The family came to Ireland in the early fourteenth century and are credited with erecting the first stone building in Galway. By 1388 one of their family, William Athy, was the Treasurer of Connacht. In later centuries George Athy (1642–1709) left Galway for America, settling in Maryland where he became a tobacco planter and also a captain in the local militia.

Blake

Claiming to descend from a knight of King Arthur's Round Table, the name 'Blake' is thought to be a corruption of the name 'Black'. The Galway Blakes came to Ireland with Richard 'Strongbow' de Clare. Richard Blake was appointed Sherriff of Connacht in 1306.

Blakes Castle was built in the 1400s as a townhouse for the prosperous family.

One branch of the Blakes was granted 12,000 acres of land in the county of Galway in 1681, including land at Ardfry, near Oranmore, on Galway Bay. In 1800 they were elevated to the peerage, when Joseph Henry Blake became Baron Wallscourt.

The eccentric John Henry Blake of Ardfry, 2nd Lord Wallscourt, married Elizabeth 'Bessie' Lock of Norbury Park, England in 1822. Something of an eccentric, he was prone to wandering the house at Ardfry naked. To spare the blushes of the servant girls,

Bessie made him carry a cowbell to alert them to his presence. The title died out in 1920, on the death of the 5th Baron.

Another branch of the Blakes owned Menlo Castle on the banks of the River Corrib.

Bodkin

Maurice Fitzgerald, son of Gerald of Windsor, also came to Ireland with Strongbow. While he settled in Wexford, his sons ventured further afield. His youngest son, Richard FitzMaurice, accompanied Richard de Burgo west of the Shannon.

Some time in the early fourteenth century an incident occurred which changed the family name. Thomas Fitz Richard, a descendant of FitzMaurice, was involved in an altercation with an Irish knight. Using a small Irish spear known as a *baudekin*, he successfully defended himself, and from then on was called 'Buaidh Baudekin' or 'Victor of the Bodkin'.

Browne

Another of the Galway families who arrived in Ireland with the first wave of Anglo-Normans were the Brownes. Philippus Browne was appointed Governor of Wexford in 1172, but his son Walter came to Galway.

One branch of Walter's descendants was elevated to the peerage in 1836, when Dominick Browne became 1st Baron Oranmore and Browne of Carrabrowne Castle, near Menlough. The castle is in ruins today. The title still exists; the 5th Baron Oranmore and Browne is the poet Dominick Browne.

D'Arcy

The D'Arcys can trace their ancestry back to France. Richard, from the Normandy village of Arci, accompanied William the Conqueror to England in 1066. The first record of them in Ireland dates from 1323, when Sir John D'Arcy was appointed Justiciar of Ireland. In the sixteenth century, Elizabeth I created James Riveagh D'Arcy Vice President of Connacht.

However, it is also possible that the name was 'Darcy', without an apostrophe, and that they were of Gaelic Irish stock. The Ó'Dorchaidhe clan of the Partry Mountains or the 'dark men' would then be their most likely origins.

They are one of the Tribes whose influence went beyond the city of Galway. Having lost land in Cromwellian times, they acquired 12,000 acres under the 1662 Act of Resettlement, which restored lands to those who had not rebelled against Cromwell but had nonetheless been punished. This land was in Connemara, where John D'Arcy built Clifden Castle in 1812 on the scenic Sky Road; the town of Clifden soon followed.

Deane

The Deanes did not arrive in Galway until the fifteenth century, later than most of the other 'Tribes'. They originated in Bristol which, as a port town, led William Allen, or Den, to Galway, where he remained presumably to exploit trade opportunities. By the sixteenth century the Deanes were trading in tobacco.

In 1667 Thomas Deane, described as a merchant, was granted 1,500 acres of land in the area of Tuam. His descendants built a fine Georgian manor house at Castlemoyle in 1770. When Ambrose Deane was declared bankrupt in 1796, the Castlemoyle Estate was bought by another of the 'Tribes', the Brownes.

Ffrench/French

The original spelling of the French family name had two *f*s, which in medieval script indicated a capital letter. They were, unsurprisingly, from France and came to Ireland with Strongbow. By 1425 Walter French had arrived in Galway.

In 1636 they bought lands in the east of Co. Galway which had once belonged to the Gaelic O'Kellys. Cromwell confiscated this estate, only for the Frenches to repurchase the land in 1702. In 1779 Charles French served as Mayor of Galway. Outside of the city they held an estate at Monivea, where they began a linen-making business in the 1700s.

Font/Faunt

Possibly of French origin, a family of Fonts were in Athenry in the early thirteenth century and they came from Leicestershire in England. They intermarried with other families of the merchant class in Galway with records showing marriages between Fonts, Athys and Kirwans.

Joyce

The first of the Joyces to come to the west of Ireland was Thomas Joyce, from Wales, towards the end of the thirteenth century. He sailed to Munster and visited the Earl of Thomond. He left Munster with a bride, Onorah O'Brien, the earl's daughter, and sailed up the west coast to Connemara. On the way there Onorah gave birth to their son, who was named MacMara ('Son of the Sea'). Thomas settled in the area then known as Iar Connacht, the western part of Connemara. MacMara married into the O'Flahertys and the Joyces were soon the dominant family in the region, giving their name to a part of Co. Galway that is still known today as 'Joyce Country'.

Kirwan

Of the fourteen 'Tribes of Galway', the Kirwans are the family with truly Irish ancestry. The modern form of the name is thought to derive from the Irish Ó'Ciardubhaín, meaning 'jet black', which was eventually anglicised to Kirwan. By the early 1400s this version of the name was in use in Galway. By the mid-seventeenth century they owned Cregg Castle at Corrandulla, but they lost this seat to the Blakes in a card game at the end of the eighteenth century.

Lynch

The most famous of the 'Tribes' are the Lynches. The French knight, Hugo de Lynch, accompanied William of Normandy to England in 1066. His descendant Andrew de Lynch followed in his footsteps of conquest when he came to Ireland with Henry II in 1171. By 1260 a John Lynch was in Galway.

Their first contribution to the town was the construction of St Nicholas' Church in 1320. Dominick Dubh Lynch FitzJohn successfully petitioned King Richard III for the grant of a charter to make Galway a city. His brother Persse became the first elected Mayor of Galway, in 1485. From then until 1654, eighty-four members of the Lynch family held that prestigious title.

The Lynches' tombs in St Nicholas' Church and their townhouse, Lynch's Castle, are all reminders of the part this family played in the building of Galway.

Martin

The name is thought to come from the Latin *cognomen* or nickname *Martinus* meaning 'warlike' and probably originated in France. Oliver Martin came to Ireland with Strongbow and later went on Crusade with Henry II's son, Richard I, the Lionheart.

The Martins were the first of the Tribes to venture beyond the protection of the city walls, buying lands in Connemara from the 'ferocious' O'Flahertys. They acquired more lands in the Act of Settlement of 1652. Later in the seventeenth century they almost lost these gains as Richard 'Nimble Dick' Martin had sided with the Jacobites in the War of the Two Kings. He visited King William III in London and pleaded his case. A trained lawyer, his nimble tongue persuaded the king to allow him to keep his estate, thus earning him his nickname. The tensions between the O'Flahertys and the Martins continued into the eighteenth century, and resulted in the murder of Nimble Dick's son Robin in 1705.

The most famous of the Martins is Richard 'Humanity Dick' Martin, the great-grandson of Nimble Dick, and founder, in 1824, of the Royal Society for the Prevention of Cruelty to Animals.

Morris

The Morris family were one of the last of the Tribes to reach Galway, first settling there as late as 1485. Little is known about where they came from.

In 1684 George Morris served on the Jacobite side of the war between James II and William of Orange.

In 1885 Michael Morris, a judge and owner of Spiddal House, became a life peer and in 1900 he was raised to the peerage, taking the title Lord Killanin.

George Henry Morris was a commanding officer with the Irish Guards during the First World War and was killed in action during the retreat from Mons on 1 September 1914. His son became the 4th Baron Killanin and served as President of the International Olympic Committee in the 1970s.

Skerritt
Robert Huscard, an Englishman, held lands in Connacht under
Richard de Burgo. By 1378, the name had evolved into Skerritt.
It is not a common name in Galway today.

LYNCH'S CASTLE

At the corner of Abbeygate Street and Shop Street is one of
Galway's most famous buildings. Lynch's Castle is the best-
preserved example of a medieval urban dwelling in Galway
and it is the oldest intact secular building in the city. While
there is no record of the exact date of its construction, it was
probably after the last major fire, which reduced Galway to
ashes in 1473. This fire was not such a bad thing, as it allowed
the merchant families to rebuild their town in stone. In fact, in
1521 Galway Corporation passed a law forbidding townspeople
from building, making or repairing any straw or thatch houses,
for fear of fire.

When first built, Lynch's Castle was probably taller than
it is today. It has been refurbished and restored many times
over its 600-year history. The most notable alteration is in the
arrangement of the windows. Originally they would have been
smaller but additional large, symmetrically placed windows in
the Georgian style were added in the eighteenth century.

The plaques, carvings and external stone features go some
way to telling the story of the original building. At the top of
the castle are a series of sixteen waterspouts which would have
drained water from the roof and directed it away from the
building. Some are carved with grotesque animal and human
heads, or gargoyles. This is a feature borrowed directly from
medieval ecclesiastical architecture.

Three round carvings depicting different coats of arms
decorate the façade of the building. A plaque on the Shop
Street side depicts the coat of arms of King Henry VII, with
an inscription in Latin which translates as 'Long Live the
King of England, France and Lord of Ireland'. This could
suggest that the building dates from the late 1480s: Henry VII
came to the throne in 1485, when he defeated Richard III

at the Battle of Bosworth. Richard had granted Galway a city charter in 1484. Perhaps this was the Lynches' way of showing their support for the new king and his dynasty.

On the Abbeygate Street side of Lynch's Castle, another stone plaque depicts the coat of arms of the Fitzgeralds of Kildare. Why this is here is unclear. It could be in recognition of the support that Gerald Fitzgerald, 8th Earl of Kildare rendered to Galway in 1504 after the Battle of Knockdoe. Ulick Burke's attack on the city prompted Fitzgerald, the Lord Deputy of Ireland, to come and put an end to Burke's quest for control of Connacht.

Another carving depicts a monkey holding a child. There is a story from medieval lore, mostly connected with the Fitzgeralds of Kildare, about a monkey saving a child from a burning building. Also depicted is the Lynch family coat of arms.

Lynch's Castle underwent significant restoration in 1930, when the building was bought by the Munster and Leinster Bank. The bank added a carved entrance to the Shop Street front. Today it is a branch of the Allied Irish Bank, the oldest building in commercial use in Ireland today.

THE LYNCH MEMORIAL

At the back of St Nicholas' Collegiate Church, on Market Street, there is a monument with a plaque commemorating an event that allegedly occurred at this site in the 1490s. The story of how Mayor James Lynch Fitzstephen hanged his own son for murder is Galway's most infamous tale.

There are various versions of the story. One version suggests that Lynch Fitzstephen sent his son, Walter, to Spain to bring home a cargo of wine. Walter spent most of the money he had been given for the transaction on the way. Rather than lose the trade, he persuaded the Spanish merchant to send his nephew to accompany Walter and the wine back to Galway to secure full payment. Walter murdered the nephew on the voyage home, throwing his body overboard. Walter's father only came to know of the terrible deed when one of the crew, who had witnessed the murder, spoke of it on his deathbed.

Another version suggests that the Spaniard was murdered for casting amorous glances at Walter Lynch's fiancée. Either way, a Spaniard had been murdered and justice had to be done. Trade between Galway and Spain could not be jeopardised. Walter was tried and found guilty of murder. In the fifteenth century the penalty for murder was death by hanging. However, nobody was willing to hang the mayor's son. And so James Lynch Fitzstephen had to do the job himself, hanging his son from the window of his home.

And what of the authenticity of the monument at the back of St Nicholas' Collegiate Church? It is a Victorian concoction of fireplaces and other stonework pilfered from the decaying buildings of Galway's medieval past.

THE CLADDAGH FISHING VILLAGE

The settlement on the west side of the Corrib, known as the Claddagh was probably there long before the Anglo-Normans arrived. From the stony shore, which gives the area its name, the fisher folk watched with trepidation as stone walls went up around the new settlement. They continued with their business of fishing in the river and the bay, and though excluded from the town, had a new market for their fish.

By the early nineteenth century it was estimated that 3,000 people lived in the settlement of 500 mud-walled, thatched cabins haphazardly arranged close together. Lining the shore were 250 Galway hookers, traditional fishing boats. Galway Bay must have been a sight to behold when the Claddagh fishing fleet took to sea, with their red sails unfurled and black hulls gliding over the choppy waters. And in the midst of the fleet, one boat would stand out. The lone white sail among the red was the privilege of the King of the Claddagh.

While the men were at sea, the women spent their days gathering bait on the seashore, mending nets and selling the fish at the Fish Market, outside the city walls in front of the Spanish Arch.

Every August, on the Sunday closest to the feast of the Assumption of the Blessed Virgin on 15 August, a Dominican priest was taken out into the bay by boat to bless the fishing fleet and to pray for all those fishing in the bay for the coming year. This tradition survives to this day, the Galway hookers now joined by modern-day trawlers.

August was an important month for the Claddagh, because it heralded the arrival of shoals of herring. As the Connemara farmers prayed for a bumper potato crop, the Claddagh fishermen prayed for seas teeming with herring. When the potato blight struck in the 1840s, decimating the potato crops, the fishermen did not fare much better. The herring stayed off the shores of Galway Bay, just beyond the reach of their boats.

The years following the Great Famine were the beginning of the end of the fishing community. As the century progressed, outsiders using new fishing methods led to the overfishing of Galway Bay. The Claddagh fishermen lost out as they did not move with the times, sticking rigidly to their traditional methods. By the early 1900s the community was in decline, the younger generation emigrating in droves. Nineteenth-century travel writers' accounts of the Claddagh suggest that the cottages were better furnished and better kept than the cottages of the tenant farmers of Connemara, but by the 1930s the Claddagh was deemed unsanitary and a health hazard. The village was eventually demolished and replaced by modern public housing.

THE CLADDAGH RING

While the village may be gone, the name lives on in another tradition of the Claddagh fishing community: the Claddagh Ring.

In the seventeenth century, Richard Joyce decided to leave Galway in search of adventure. He boarded a ship and headed for Spain. He got more than he bargained for when he was captured by the Moors and sold into slavery, ending up in Algiers. For fourteen years he was the slave of a goldsmith. He learnt the craft and returned to Galway in the 1690s, when he was released from slavery in a deal brokered by King William III to free English and Irish subjects in Algiers.

With a trade under his belt, Joyce was soon making a particular type of ring for the fishermen of the Claddagh. At its centre is a heart symbolising love, clasped either side by a hand.

A crown sits on top of the heart. Wearing the ring with the tip of the heart pointing towards the finger nail indicated that a lady was betrothed. On marriage, the ring was turned around and served as a wedding ring, the heart now pointing towards her own heart, suggesting that it was closed to anyone other than her husband.

Still crafted in Galway today, Claddagh rings are a unique symbol of Galway.

EYRE SQUARE

Today Eyre Square is at the heart of the modern city of Galway, but it was not always so. Eyre Square was once an open green space outside the main gates of the walled town. In the late medieval period the town's gallows were located on the green, and it was also an ideal space for fairs and markets, which continued up until the twentieth century.

In 1712 the Mayor of Galway, Edward Eyre, granted the land to the people of Galway for use as a public park. By 1801, the Green, as it was known, was used as a military training ground by General Meyrick, and for a time it was called Meyrick Square. The name did not stick and from the 1820s it was commonly referred to as Eyre Square. In the 1840s new wrought-iron railings enclosed the central area, and it finally became the public park of the modern city centre.

One of the main features of Eyre Square in the late nineteenth century was a statue of Lord Dunkellin. Sculpted in bronze by John Henry Foley, it was erected to the memory of the eldest son of Ulick John de Burgh, 14th Earl of Clanricarde. Lord Dunkellin was a soldier in the British Army. He was captured at Sebastopol during the Crimean War but was released on the orders of the Tsar of Russia – his father had served as British Ambassador to Russia at the end of the 1830s.

Lord Dunkellin became a Member of Parliament for Galway in 1865, but died in 1867 with no heir. The estate passed to his younger brother, who notoriously became known as 'Lord Clanrackrent'. The Clanricarde tenants were asked to contribute money for the memorial statue, which stood on Eyre Square until 1922. In that year, the British left Ireland and the statue was seen as a symbol of landlordism and British rule. It was pulled down, dragged to the river and thrown into the fast-flowing waters, apparently while a band played the tune 'I'm forever blowing bubbles'.

The statue that most people associate with Eyre Square is that of Pádraic Ó'Conaire (1882–1928), who wrote in the Irish language. The plaque accompanying the statue described Ó'Conaire as a 'true Irishman and renowned author'. Designed by Albert Power, the statue was unveiled by Eamon de Valera in 1935. For the next seventy or so years people sat on him, had their photographs taken with him and sadly some saw fit to vandalise him. After the statue was decapitated in 1999 it was moved to the Galway City Museum.

Most of the buildings around Eyre Square date from the nineteenth century, the most imposing of which is the Meyrick Hotel on the south side of the square. The hotel was built between 1851 and 1853 by the Midland and Great Western Railway Company, conveniently beside the new railway station. Originally called the Railway Hotel, it later became the Great Southern Hotel. Today its name recalls the former name for the square, which it overlooks.

In 1905 a relic of Galway's Tribes was moved to the north side of Eyre Square. Browne's Gateway had originally been the entrance to Browne's Castle, the seventeenth-century townhouse of the merchant Browne family on Abbeygate Street. Carved into the door are the Browne and Lynch coats of arms,

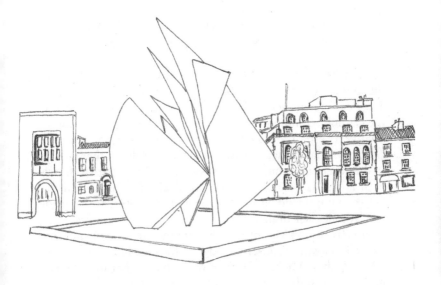

commemorating the marriage of Martin Browne and Marie Lynch in 1627.

In 1957 a statue of Liam Mellowes, who led the Galway members of the Irish Volunteers during the 1916 Easter Rising, was erected on the north side of Eyre Square.

The 1960s brought further changes to Eyre Square. To make way for parking, the railings were removed and reused to surround St Nicholas' Collegiate Church. The gardens underwent a refurbishment. When they were reopened in 1965 they were called the John Fitzgerald Kennedy Memorial Gardens, after the assassinated President of the United States of America who had visited Galway in June 1963.

In 1984 the sculptor Eamon O'Doherty was commissioned to create a monument of a uniquely Galway symbol to commemorate Galway's 500th year as a city. His fountain recreates the sails of a Galway hooker, the traditional fishing boat of Galway Bay.

Today no cars are parked around Eyre Square and the west side is pedestrianised. And once again, if only at Christmas, it is used as a marketplace.

ROMAN CATHOLIC CATHEDRAL OF OUR LADY ASSUMED INTO HEAVEN AND ST NICHOLAS OF MYRA

In 1816 the Protestant Mayor of Galway, Hyacinth Daly, laid the foundation stone for St Nicholas' Roman Catholic Church. The Penal Laws were still in place, but had been relaxed and the Catholic community of Galway finally had a parish church. Two years after Catholic Emancipation, in 1831, the Catholic Diocese of Galway was created. A diocese needs a cathedral, but in the absence of funds to build one, the existing parish church of St Nicholas became the pro-cathedral. In 1876 fundraising began, but it would be another ninety years before Galway got its Catholic cathedral.

In 1909 Bishop McCormack bought the site of an old military barracks close to O'Brien's Bridge in the city. However, by the 1930s Bishop Michael Browne was advised that the site was no longer suitable. Times had changed, a bigger church was needed and the O'Brien's Bridge site would not have any room for parking. However, a new, more suitable site became available in 1939.

The government of the day planned to demolish Galway's Old Jail, which was located across the Salmon Weir Bridge from the Court House. The land was transferred to the Bishop of Galway for the purpose of building a new cathedral. It did not escape the Galwegians' notice that the purpose of the site was being transferred from sinners to saints!

The outbreak of the Second World War led to further delays. Cardinal D'Alton finally laid the foundation stone on 27 October 1957 at a ceremony attended by bishops from all over Ireland, the President of Ireland, Sean T. O'Kelly, and the Taoiseach John A. Costello.

Pope Pius XII approved the plans of Dublin architect John J. Robinson. Sisk and Co. Ltd were contracted to build the church for £600,000. On 14 August 1965, Cardinal Cushing of Boston said the first Mass in the new cathedral. The following day was the Feast of the Assumption of our Blessed Lady into Heaven and the cathedral was dedicated to her and to St Nicholas of Myra, the patron saint of mariners and a saint long

associated with Galway. The church nevertheless came to be known as Galway Cathedral, although local jokers at the time dubbed it the 'Taj Micháel', after Bishop Micháel Browne.

The vast interior's limestone walls are decorated with marble and stained-glass windows. The upper windows of the nave, some of which were completed as recently as 1999, depict stories from the Old Testament, and the lower windows depict the life of Christ as told in the New Testament. The north, east and west rose windows depict the joyful, sorrowful and glorious mysteries of the rosary respectively.

St Nicholas Chapel in the cathedral has a link between the old and new churches of Galway. Imbedded in the wall is a stone triptych of carved figures representing Our Blessed Lady and the Blessed Trinity of the Father, Son and Holy Spirit. The carvings are seventeenth-century and were originally located in the vestry of St Nicholas' Collegiate Church. In the late eighteenth century the warden of the church had them removed and ordered that they be thrown into the sea. A Catholic priest met the carter tasked with the disposal of the triptych and persuaded him to bring them instead to the Catholic parish church, which later became the pro-cathedral. They were placed on a wall there until they were again moved, this time to the new cathedral. These figures have watched over Galway's faithful since the seventeenth century.

3

THE BUILT HERITAGE OF COUNTY GALWAY

From ancient times people have used stone to construct places in which to shelter, work and worship. Thanks to their skill and the durability of stone, their built legacy remains. The history of Ireland can be traced through its built heritage, of which Co. Galway has superb examples, from ancient forts to round towers, ruined abbeys to stately homes.

PREHISTORIC GALWAY

The most intriguing built heritage is that from prehistoric times. The often partial remains, which have stood for millennia, are the legacy of a time when nothing was written down, leaving future generations to guess who built them and why.

Dun Aengus

While it is not the only ancient stone fort on the Aran Islands, Dun Aengus is the most spectacular, perched on a cliff edge 60m (200ft) above the Atlantic Ocean. Its builders must have thought they were building on the edge of the world when they chose this spot on the coast of Inishmore.

Legend suggests that the fort was built by the mythical Fir Bolg, the original inhabitants of Ireland. They were defeated by the Tuatha Dé Dannan, a mystical tribe. The Fir Bolg either fled or were banished to the Aran Islands, where they built an impenetrable fort named after their chieftain, Aengus.

Dun Aengus, Aengus's Fort, is thought to date from 1100 BC, but it may have been enhanced between 700 BC and AD 400. The main fort is a semi-circular dry stone wall, open on the cliff edge, a natural defence. The walls here are 3.7m (12ft) high. Outside this wall are two more semi-circular walls, and a fourth some distance beyond these. Between these last two walls is a further defence known as a *cheveaux de frise*. This ancient defence is made up of hundreds of stone stakes firmly embedded in the ground and pointing in different directions, making it impossible to attack the fort on foot or horseback. Whoever built Dun Aengus, they were determined that it would not be taken.

Dun Aengus is not the only such fort on the Aran Islands. Dun Dubhchathair, or the Black Fort, also boasts a *cheveaux de frise* and may have been built around the same time as Dun Aengus. Dun Eochla, built on the highest point of Inishmore, and Dun Onaght are smaller, circular or oval forts built inland. Dun Conor on Inishmaan is an oval fort, and although smaller than Dun Aengus, it has thicker walls.

Crannogs

Crannogs are artificial islands built from wood and found on lakes throughout Ireland and Scotland. Almost 1,500 have been identified in Ireland. Though difficult to date, crannogs first appear in the British Isles from the Bronze Age and were in use up to early medieval times. The name 'crannog' was first used in the twelfth century. It translates as 'young tree', possibly referring to recently abandoned artificial islands then covered in saplings.

A number of lakes in Galway have crannogs. As recently as 2010, due to dropping water levels, a crannog was found on Lough Dhúleitir near Carna. Loughrea Lake has thirteen crannogs, some of which are visible from the shoreline. Some are completely submerged, suggesting that the water level was once lower. Spearheads found on the Loughrea crannogs suggest that they date from the Bronze Age. A dagger dating from the Middle Ages suggests that they were inhabited until then.

One explanation for the existence of crannogs suggests that by surrounding themselves with water, the occupants were protected from the wolves and bears that roamed ancient

Ireland. A palisade would have surrounded each island, inside of which were wattle-and-mud huts for accommodation. A boat or a partially submerged causeway provided access from the shore. Another theory suggests that because Ireland was covered in dense forest, clearing an area with primitive tools would have been a laborious process. Building an artificial island not only provided security; it also allowed a view of the sky.

ECCLESIASTICAL ARCHITECTURE

St Patrick began his mission of converting the pagan Irish to Christianity in AD 432. Ever since, holy men have built churches in which to worship across Ireland. From simple unadorned churches built on sites founded by early saints, such as St Ronan and St Enda on the Aran Islands, to the Celtic-influenced interior of St Brendan's Cathedral in Loughrea, Co. Galway boasts centuries of ecclesiastical architecture.

Kilmacduagh Round Tower
Is there a more iconic Celtic structure than the Irish round tower? Rising up from a collection of ruined buildings, with the grey hills of the Burren as a backdrop, is the round tower of Kilmacduagh. In the seventh century, St Colman was wandering in this area when his girdle slipped from his waist to the ground. He decided to build a monastery at that spot. By the thirteenth century, Kilmacduagh was a diocese (it has since merged with the Diocese of Galway) and a cathedral and bishop's house were built at the site.

The round tower, however, is older and dates from AD 1000. School children were taught that the early Christian monks built these tall thin towers as a place of refuge from the raiding Vikings. Since the towers were the tallest man-made structures in the landscape at the time and would have served as a useful landmark directing the Vikings to their prey, it is more likely that they originally served as bell towers from which to summon the monks to prayer.

The doorway was always high off the ground and reached with a ladder. Had the monks breached the structure further down, the tower would have toppled over. An internal wooden

staircase would have enabled a monk to reach the top window to ring a bell.

There are a number of features that make the round tower at Kilmacduagh one of the most important in the country. At 34m (111ft) it is the tallest. It has a circumference of 17m (56ft) and walls 2m (6.5ft) thick. With eleven, Kilmacduagh has more windows than any other round tower in Ireland. The positioning of its door is also unusual. At a height of 7m (23ft) above the ground, the door is higher than any other. But most interesting of all, the tower leans off-centre by 75cm (2ft) towards the south-west.

In 1870, Sir William Gregory of Coole Park had the tower's conical top restored.

Clonfert Cathedral

St Brendan the Navigator founded a monastery at Clonfert in AD 563. He died at Annaghdown in AD 577, and was buried at Clonfert. The Synod of Rathbreasail in 1111 recognised the ecclesiastical significance of Clonfert and declared it a diocese. A small, simple rectangular cathedral was built. Some time in the 1160s an ornate west door was added, carved in the Hiberno-Romanesque style.

The use of rounded Romanesque arches first came to Ireland in the early twelfth century. Irish masons were soon embellishing the arches of doors and windows with carvings, in the belief that it would please God. To further enhance their buildings, masons gave depth to their arches by creating orders or tiers. This style is unique to Ireland. A group of masons known as the 'School of the West' found inspiration for the elaborate carvings and sculptures on the orders of arches in the native flora and fauna.

At Clonfert the narrow west door is surrounded by a sandstone Romanesque arch of six orders, each of which is heavily carved. The supports and curves of each order are carved with foliage, zigzags, animals and human figures. Above the arches is an arcade of five smaller rounded arches, each surrounding a human head. A steeply pitched pediment mounts the arcade and this triangular shape is divided into smaller triangles, with a head in each inverted triangle.

Illustration by Maia Dunne

Considering that the arch has been exposed to the wet west of Ireland climate for over 900 years, its carvings are in good condition. Today the church serves as the cathedral for the Church of Ireland Diocese of Clonfert.

Romanesque Arch at St Mary's Church of Ireland Cathedral Tuam
Co. Galway can boast a second fine example of the Hiberno-Romanesque arch. Tuam's Church of Ireland Cathedral houses the widest one in Ireland, with a span of 5.5m (18ft).

In the fifth century St Jarlath was travelling in the area when the wheel of his chariot broke. He took this as a sign from God and founded a monastery on the site, which would later become the town of Tuam. He later became the first Bishop there.

To mark the elevation of Tuam to an archdiocese in 1152, Turlough O'Connor, the High King of Ireland whose seat of power was in Tuam, had a cathedral built. The surviving feature of that building is the Hiberno-Romanesque arch which spanned the chancel. The arch has five ornately carved orders. This arch and the three Romanesque windows of the chancel were incorporated into a new cathedral, built on the site in the fourteenth century.

A third cathedral was commissioned for the Church of Ireland in the nineteenth century. The architect, Sir Thomas Deane, was given the task of enlarging the old church and incorporating the twelfth-century arch and chancel. Because the arch has been indoors, it has not suffered erosion and the carvings are as clear as the day they were first hewn from the original sandstone eight and a half centuries ago.

Clontuskert Abbey, Augustinian (c. 1180)
The Norman Conquest of the twelfth century brought with it monastic orders from Europe intent on bringing the Celtic Christian Church in Ireland into line with the Roman Church. Soon the Augustinians, Cistercians and Dominicans were busy building and preaching throughout Ireland. They came to the newly founded towns of Athenry, Loughrea and Portumna. Some monks chose to build their monasteries in parts of the county not yet settled. Today most of those monastic sites are ruins, abandoned by their holy men in the sixteenth century when Henry VIII's Dissolution of the Monasteries shut them down.

The Canons Regular of St Augustine, a secular order, was the first of the continental orders to cross the Shannon. At the invitation of the Gaelic O'Kellys, they built their first western monastery at Clontuskert, today on the main Ballinasloe–Portumna road. Little is known about the early history of the monastery, thought to have been founded in 1180. It was struck by lightning and burnt down in 1404, leading to a major rebuild. Much of what remains today dates from this period.

To finance the refurbishment the monks offered ten-year indulgences to their congregation. The monks put the money they collected to good use. The east window of the church is a complex interweave of stone. The impressive vaulted ceiling, rood screen and cloister arcade have all survived the ravages of time. The west door of the church is particularly worthy of mention. The inscription over the door reads:

> Mathew by the Grace of God, Bishop of Clonfert, and Patrick O'Naughton, canon of this house, caused me to be made in 1471.

The good bishop and his canon decided that the door should be adorned with the figures of St Michael, St John the Baptist, St Catherine and the figure of a bishop, with his foot on a snake, which suggests St Patrick.

The earls of Clanricarde were given the monastery in 1551. Their ownership ensured that monks were able to live and pray here until the end of the seventeenth century, long after Henry VIII had ordered the closure of monasteries in the mid-sixteenth century. Eventually, Clontuskert Abbey was abandoned and fell into ruin.

Ross Errily Abbey, Franciscan (1400)

Between Headford and Ballinrobe, in a flat landscape devoid of landmarks, the ruin of Ross Errily Abbey, the largest Franciscan ruin in Ireland, suddenly appears in the distance.

The actual date of its foundation is unclear, but it was most likely built around 1400. The castellated bell tower, a common feature of Franciscan monasteries, is the focal point of this impressive ruin. The church layout is typical of the time: the tower is centred over the nave, the altar is at the east end of the nave and the main entrance at its west end. The west door of Ross Errily is off-centre, an unusual feature for a monastery of this period.

The domestic buildings, on the north side of the church, are extensive. The kitchens are large, the remains of chimneys indicating the location of ovens. In one corner can be seen a stone tank which was used for keeping fish alive and fresh for Friday. In the Refectory Hall, the reader's desk still stands. A monk would have read scripture from the desk as his fellow monks sat and ate in silence.

The earls of Clanricarde were granted the abbey in 1562. They protected the monks, and attempts to close it down completely were never successful. The monks would leave in time of persecution, such as in 1656 when Cromwell's soldiers took over the monastery, but they always returned – that is until 1753, when they left for good, leaving this fine example of a Franciscan abbey to fall into ruin.

St Brendan's Cathedral Loughrea

Following the Catholic Emancipation Act of 1829, a new wave of ecclesiastical building began in Ireland. The foundation stone for St Brendan's Cathedral in Loughrea was laid in 1897. The exterior of St Brendan's Cathedral does not prepare the visitor for the treasures within. Built at the height of the Celtic Revival, the cathedral is a gallery of Celtic Revival art, thanks mainly to the efforts of Edward Martyn and the local clergy. Between them they set about transforming the blank interiors into something special: a church decorated by Irish artists and inspired by the artistry of Ireland's Celtic past.

Edward Martyn was a local landowner involved in the Celtic Literary Revival movement. When he began looking for stained-glass windows for Labane church, he found that nothing was available in Ireland and imports were of an inferior quality. He eventually commissioned the English stained glass artist Christopher Whall to design the windows, who sent his pupil Alfred Ernest Child to install them. Martyn was so impressed with the windows that he persuaded Whall to allow Child to stay in Ireland, where he began training artists in the craft. Along with the portrait painter Sarah Purser, Child founded a stained glass studio,

An Túr Gloine ('The Glass Tower'). The studio would provide all of the stained-glass windows for St Brendan's Cathedral.

From 1904 A.E. Child, Sarah Purser and their pupils at An Túr Gloine designed, painted and executed the windows for St Brendan's. However, the first windows to be installed were designed by Christopher Whall. The three sanctuary windows depicting the Annunciation, the Agony in the Garden and the Resurrection (all 1903) were not original to Loughrea. Whall based them on designs he had used the previous year in the south-west transept window at Canterbury Cathedral.

Although a portrait painter by profession, Sarah Purser turned her hand to stained glass, designing a number of the windows, most notably those depicting St Ita (1904) in the baptistry, the Nativity window (1912) in the east transept and St Brendan in the porch.

Micheal Healy was the first student taken on by An Túr Gloine. Trained by Child, his first window, St Simeon (1904), shows a similar style to his master. However, over the next four decades,

Healy's progression from pupil to master can be traced in the works he created for St Brendan's.

Healy developed his own unique style, which culminated in his final and most spectacular window, the Last Judgement (1941). Located in the west transept, it has been described as one of the crowning masterpieces of the stained glass revival. Other artists who joined An Túr Gloine and created windows for St Brendan's were Evie Hone, a pupil of Healy's, Hubert McGoldrick and Beatrice Elvery.

But the stained-glass windows are only part of the Celtic Revival decoration of

St Brendan's. Once the cathedral was ready for worship, the interior architectural work was taken over by William A. Scott, a young, unknown architect. He designed all the wrought-iron work throughout St Brendan's, which was forged locally, a process admired by T.S. Eliot, who visited the foundry while in Co Galway. Each of the 109 pews has an individual carving.

The sculptor John Hughes, best known for the statue of Queen Victoria which once sat outside Leinster House, created the beautiful Virgin and Child marble statue in the side chapel. He also created the bronze relief over the main altar, the Man of Sorrows.

Edward Martyn wanted simple wooden crosses to represent the Stations of the Cross. However, after he died it was decided that Ethel Rhind, another An Túr Gloine artist, should create a set of Stations. She was an expert in the opus sectile mosaic style and had created a set of Stations for St Enda's Church in Spiddal. The set she created in Loughrea are very similar.

New altar furnishings were put in place in the 1980s. To commemorate the centenary of the cathedral in 2002, sculptor Thomas Glendon carved two pillar heads that had been untouched, completing a set of the Four Evangelists which had been begun by the sculptor Michael Shortall. The latest works have kept the traditions started back in the early 1900s: Irish artists creating Celtic-inspired pieces to adorn the best ecclesiastical example of Celtic Revival art in Ireland.

CASTLES AND COUNTRY HOUSES

Along with bringing the monastic orders to Ireland, the Anglo-Normans introduced the concept of building sturdy stone castles and tower houses. The hostility of the Gaelic chieftains meant that they needed buildings which could be easily defended. They were also making a statement: 'We are here to stay.' Remains of these tower houses can be seen throughout Ireland. Galway has two fine examples in the castles of Athenry and Aughnanure.

By the 1600s Continental architectural influences had reached Ireland. Portumna Castle is one of the best examples of the transition from fortified house to manor house.

The golden age of the 'big house' was the eighteenth century. The Gregorys of Coole Park and the D'Arcys of Kiltullagh are examples of families who built comfortable Georgian houses in Co. Galway. However, these houses were not on the scale of those being built in the east, such as Russborough in Co. Wicklow or Cartron in Co. Kildare. The Great Famine was the beginning of the end for many of these houses.

By 1870 Co. Galway had more landlords per head of population than any other county in Ireland. The Land League campaigned for a fairer distribution of land. The Land Acts of the late 1800s required the gentry to sell land to their tenants. Some of the big houses were abandoned and, like the abbeys before them, fell into ruin. Killtullagh House is a poignant example of a ruined 'big house', its two chimneys rising from the shell of the once-beautiful mansion. Some, such as Roxborough and Spiddal House, were burnt in the 1920s because they were seen as symbols of the oppressive years of landlordism and others, like Coole Park, were demolished.

Despite all this, the 1800s saw the building of two spectacular houses in Co. Galway: Kylemore and Ashford.

Athenry Castle (c. 1235)

Meiler de Bermingham founded the town of Athenry in 1235. The 'Ford of the Kings' was on the route of the Esker Riada, a gravel ridge crossing Ireland from east to west. His was one of the first castles built in Connacht.

It was built from rough stone. The only cut stone in the castle surrounds the door and the windows. Ornamental carvings decorate these, a trend more common in churches than the dwellings of the period. The only door allowing access to the castle is on the second floor, and was reached by a wooden staircase. Another feature, unusual in a castle of the period, is the canopy over the doorway.

Originally, Athenry Castle was a two-storey building. An additional storey and gables were added in the fifteenth century. The interior would have been dark and cold. As there were no chimneys, the only heat came from a fire lit in the uppermost room. The smoke was extracted through a vent in the roof. A protective curtain wall surrounds the castle.

ATHENRY CASTLE

By the sixteenth century the de Berminghams had had enough of the cold, smoky castle and abandoned it for more comfortable quarters. The castle fell into disrepair, but was restored by the Office of Public Works in the 1990s.

Aughnanure Castle

During the medieval period over 200 tower houses were built in Co. Galway. The best-preserved of these is Aughnanure Castle, near Oughterard. It was built around 1500 by the O'Flathertys, one of the oldest Galway families. They were of Gaelic stock and had once been the bane of the Tribes of Galway. A sign over the west gate of Galway city in the Middle Ages read, 'From the ferocious O'Flathertys, Good Lord, deliver us.'

Aughnanure was built for one purpose only: defence. It is the tallest tower house of its kind in Ireland, with six storeys. In the battlements are machicolations, stone structures protruding from the walls, with a hole in the floor, which allowed for hot oil or arrows to be rained down on attackers. At two corners on the third storey of the castle are bartizans, overhanging turrets where an archer would have been positioned to fire through the arrow slits. A commanding view over Lough Corrib meant that invaders from the water could be seen in advance. If they reached the castle, it was surrounded with a double 'bawn' or walled courtyard complete with a watchtower, as a further defence.

The castle passed in and out of the O'Flahertys' hands over the centuries. The last O'Flaherty left Aughnanure as recently as 1952, when the Office of Public Works acquired the castle.

Portumna Castle

Portumna Castle, on the shores of Lough Derg, is one of the most important castles in Ireland. It marks the transition from the fortified tower house, built for defence, to the grand manor house built for comfort and show. The 4th Earl of Clanricarde built Portumna Castle in the Jacobean style in 1618. It is one of the first buildings in Ireland to use features made popular during the Italian Renaissance.

Portumna Castle has towers at each corner of a central block. The building is symmetrical, with three bays either side of a central doorway, which is ornately decorated and reached by a sweeping staircase. The arrow slits of earlier castles have been replaced by larger mullioned windows. Chimneys mean that rooms could be heated without the smothering effects of trapped smoke. Another new feature is the classically decorated arched gateway leading to an ornamental garden in the forecourt of the castle.

Despite the move to making the building more comfortable and visibly more attractive, Portumna Castle still has defensive features. Battlements on the roof are completed with a machicolation directly above the front door. Gun ports ensure that the castle could be defended if attackers managed to breach the protective outer walls.

Although the 4th Earl of Clanricarde is thought to have never visited his new castle, subsequent earls did live there. When the castle was burnt down in 1826, the family took up residence in converted estate buildings close to its gutted ruins. Construction of a new stately home began in the 1860s but it was never finished.

By the 1960s Portumna Castle was a roofless shell. The Office of Public Works took ownership of the castle in 1968 and has since undertaken a programme of conservation work. Today the ground floor is open to the public.

Ashford Castle

Straddling the borders of Co. Galway and Co. Mayo, there has been a castle on the shores of Lough Corrib at Ashford since 1228. Richard de Burgo built the first tower castle here and the lands stayed in the de Burgos' control until the seventeenth century, when the lands were granted to the Brownes, one of the Galway Tribes. In 1715 they built a shooting lodge close to the lake.

The difficult years of the Famine meant that by 1850, the 1st Lord Oranmore and Browne was bankrupt. Under the Encumbered Estate Act he had to sell the Ashford estate. Sir Benjamin Lee Guinness of the famous brewing family bought it. He added a French-style chateau to the existing buildings. His son, Arthur Edward Guinness, rebuilt the entire west side of Ashford Castle in the 1870s in the new gothic style popular at the time.

Arthur sold his interest in the Guinness brewery to his younger brother to pursue a career in politics. He was elevated to the peerage in 1880 as Lord Ardilaun, taking the name from the island 'Ard Álainn' on Lough Corrib. Lord Ardilaun spent his winters at Ashford hosting shooting parties. The Prince of Wales, later King George V, stayed there as a guest of the Guinnesses in 1908.

The house and estate were sold again in the 1930s and converted into a hotel. Today Ashford Castle is one of the most prestigious hotels in Ireland. Guests have included Prince Rainier and Princess Grace of Monaco, John Lennon and Ronald Reagan. The actor Pierce Brosnan was married there in 2001, as was the golfer Rory McIlroy, in 2017.

Kylemore Abbey

Kylemore Abbey is one of the most impressive country houses in Ireland. The granite mansion rises out of a clearing and is often reflected in the tranquil waters of Pollacappul Lough.

Mitchell Henry, a Harley Street surgeon, and his wife Margaret honeymooned in Connemara in the 1840s, and were so taken with the beauty of the region that in the 1860s they bought 13,000 acres of land at Kylemore, intending to build themselves a country house. Henry gave up his practice to take over the family's cotton business in Manchester and enter politics. He was suitably wealthy to fund the building of a mansion in the wilds of Connemara.

Work began on their neo-Gothic mansion in 1866. Granite was brought by sea from a quarry at Dalkey near Dublin. Most of the labour came from the local area, providing much-needed jobs in a region devoid of industry. The house boasted a room for every purpose: a dining room, a morning room, a library, a smoking room, a billiards room, a ballroom, four living rooms, four bathrooms and thirty-three bedrooms to accommodate the steady stream of guests.

The Victorian walled garden had glasshouses and hot houses, growing exotic fruits such as figs and bananas. All the produce was for use in the 'big house'.

Once construction was complete, Kylemore continued to provide employment for the locals as maids, gardeners and workmen were all needed to keep the estate running. Kylemore even had its own fire engine.

Mitchell Henry also built a church at Kylemore: a neo-Gothic chapel based on Norwich Cathedral, decorated inside with Irish marble and polished stone.

After Margaret died of dysentery in Egypt in 1874, Mitchell Henry moved back to London and eventually sold Kylemore. It came into the hands of the Duke of Manchester in 1900, but he found it too costly to maintain and defaulted on the mortgage. It was taken over by a bank.

In 1914 an enclosed order of Benedictine nuns at Ypres in Belgium had to abandon their convent as the First World War raged around them. They moved to England and then Ireland, hoping that some day they could return home. Sadly, their Belgian convent was damaged beyond repair and in 1920 they paid £45,000 for Kylemore House, which they renamed Kylemore Abbey. In 1932 they erected a statue of Christ on the hill overlooking Kylemore in thanksgiving for their new sanctuary.

The nuns opened an international boarding school at Kylemore, which they ran until 2010. They have since used their entrepreneurial skills to make Kylemore Abbey the most popular visitor attraction in Galway.

CONNECTING GALWAY TO THE REST OF THE WORLD

In 1822 the Scottish civil engineer Alexander Nimmo arrived in the west of Ireland, tasked with bringing new infrastructures to Connemara which would make it more accessible and support commerce in the region. He designed and built piers along the coast, and planned a canal which would bypass the fast-flowing Corrib and make Lough Corrib navigable to the sea (this was never built). He planned and built the road network that runs through Connemara.

In 1815, Charles Bianconi, an Italian emigrant living in Clonmel, began operating a horse-drawn carriage service between Clonmel and Cahir. The Napoleonic Wars were over and he was able to buy up many of the cheap horses that flooded the market and employ their now redundant handlers. By 1837 the carriage service had reached Galway. Taking advantage of Nimmo's roads, Bianconi's cars took ten hours to travel from Galway to Clifden carrying mail and passengers. This service ran until the 1890s, when it was replaced with a railway service.

Dublin to Galway

The first railway line in Ireland ran from Dublin to Dun Laoghaire and was opened in 1834. By the 1840s, Acts of Parliament were being passed to allow railway companies to develop further lines throughout Ireland. The Midland Great Western Railway Company was granted permission and funding for a connection to link Galway to Dublin, via Mullingar. The route included a bridge over the Shannon at Athlone. By 1851 the Galway line was open for business. In addition to carrying passengers and mail, the service also carried livestock from the west to the ports of Dublin for export to Britain.

The main stops on the route through Co. Galway were at Ballinasloe, Woodlawn and Athenry. Lord Ashtown had provided land for the railway to run through his estate and in return was given a railway station close to Woodlawn House.

By 1897, four trains a day were operating each way between Galway and Dublin. The mail train left Dublin at 7 a.m. and arrived at Galway just under four hours later. The mainline from Dublin to Galway still operates and works to a timetable not dissimilar to the one used when the line opened in 1851, although the journey is much faster today.

Limerick to Sligo

By 1860 another railway was running through the county. The Waterford, Limerick and Western Railway operated a line from Limerick to Sligo, which went through Gort, Ardrahan, Craughwell, Athenry, Ballyglunin and continued on to Tuam. Ballyglunin railway station featured in the 1952 film *The Quiet Man*. This line was eventually closed to passengers in the 1960s but continued to transport livestock until the 1980s. In recent years part of the line linking Ennis to Craughwell has been reopened.

Loughrea Attymon Light Rail

The Transway Act of 1883 allowed for the construction of branch lines from the main railways. The Loughrea Attymon Light Railway linked Loughrea to the main Galway–Dublin line at Attymon. It was described as a 'baronial line' in reference to the units of local government at the time, before county councils came into existence in 1898.

The Loughrea Attymon Light Railway opened in 1890, carrying passengers the 14.5km (9 miles) from Loughrea to Attymon, where they could meet the Galway- or Dublin-bound trains. When it was closed in 1975, the Loughrea Attymon Light Railway was the last branch line operating in Ireland. Today, part of the new link road that connects Loughrea to the M6 motorway follows the route of the old railway line and joins the motorway at Dunsandle, the only stop between Loughrea and Attymon, where timber from the Dunsandle Estate was once loaded on to train carriages.

Galway to Clifden
By the late nineteenth century, the railways were opening Ireland up to commerce and trade. However, Connemara was still remote and inaccessible. The road network was poor and sea transport was still the main means of transporting people and goods from Connemara to Galway. This was unreliable as harsh winter weather often disrupted travel. In 1891 the Midland Great Western Railway Company began work on the Galway to Clifden Railway. Initially it was suggested that the route should follow the coast, as this was where the majority of the 60,000-strong population of Connemara lived, and the railway would be of use in developing the fishing industry. However, the powers that be decided on an inland route that almost followed the line of Alexander Nimmo's road. The landowners of Connemara, who provided land for the track and would benefit from easier access to their estates, had some influence on the chosen route.

The first leg of the route to Oughterard opened on New Year's Day in 1895 and by July the train ran all the way to Clifden via Moycullen, Rosscahill, Oughterard, Maam Cross, Recess and Ballynahinch. The 77km (48 miles) line had cost £9,000 per mile at a time when the average cost of building a mile of railway elsewhere was £4,000. The costs mounted because a tunnel had to be dug under Prospect Hill in Galway city, and a viaduct was needed to span the Corrib. The boggy terrain of Connemara also posed challenges for the railway builders.

The line never brought as much commerce to Connemara as was hoped. It did, however, open up the region to tourists. Between 1903 and 1906 a service left Dublin at midday and

arrived in Clifden at 5 p.m., allowing those interested in shooting and fishing to stop off at hotels, such as that built at Recess. In 1903, King Edward VII and his queen, Alexandra, lunched at Recess before boarding the train to Galway.

The line eventually closed in 1935. The granite stumps of the Galway–Clifden Viaduct are still in situ in the River Corrib and the embankments of the old line can be seen along the route of the N59 in Connemara. The old station house at Clifden is now a bar.

Marconi Station

Guglielmo Marconi, the Italian pioneer of wireless communication, came to Ireland in 1905 in search of a site on which to build a new transatlantic wireless station. His station at Poldhu in Cornwall had begun communicating with Newfoundland in 1901, but he was having difficulties extending the service to Nova Scotia. He came further west and discovered a suitable site 3 miles outside Clifden on the Derrygimlagh Bog.

There were a number of factors that made the Clifden site ideal for Marconi's station. To begin with, it offered a direct, uninterrupted line across the Atlantic to the Canadian coastline. Clifden had a willing and able workforce and was accessible by train. The pier at Clifden was convenient for bringing in heavy equipment to the site by sea. Finally the Derrygimlagh

Bog provided a ready source of fuel for generating the electricity needed for the operation.

The extensive buildings on the site included a boiler house, electricity generating hall, a transmission room and staff quarters. The most imposing structures were the eight transmission masts, which were about 60m (200ft) tall. Once transmission began, the masts would have been alive with sparks flying, lighting up the night sky over the bog.

The station began transmitting communications to Glace Bay in Nova Scotia on 17 October 1907. At its peak, it employed 350 people, some 200 of whom were seasonal workers cutting and gathering turf. In 1922, during the Civil War, the station was burnt down. It closed permanently shortly afterwards, leaving the buildings to crumble.

Marconi was from Bologna, but had Irish connections. His mother was Annie Jameson, of the Irish whiskey family. His first wife was Beatrice O'Brien of Dromoland Castle.

4

THE PEOPLE OF GALWAY

The local people of a region build the towns, generate the economy and over centuries of activity they create history, stories and culture. From a once-populous county of 440,000 in 1841 to its much-reduced population of 250,000 today, Galway has provided its fair share of interesting and sometimes famous people. A list of Galway's great and good includes feisty women, eccentric aristocrats, brave soldiers and conscientious priests.

PEOPLE BORN IN GALWAY

Nora Barnacle, Wife of James Joyce (1884–1951)
Nora was born in Galway in 1884. Her father, Thomas Barnacle, was a baker and her mother, Annie Hanoria Healy, a dressmaker. The family lived at 4 Bowling Green, but Nora was sent to live with her maternal grandmother, a common practice at the time. She attended the Convent of Mercy in Newtownsmith until the age of 13 and then worked as a laundress. In 1904 she left for Dublin and found work as a live-in chambermaid at Finn's Hotel. The hotel is long gone, but its faded name on the red-brick gable wall is still visible from Nassau Street.

It was here on 10 June that Nora met the writer James Joyce. He later immortalised their first romantic meeting, which occurred six days later, in *Ulysses*. The novel follows the exploits of Leopold Bloom as he wanders around Dublin on 16 June 1904. The character of Molly Bloom is based on Nora.

In October of that year they eloped to Austria, but didn't actually get married. They spent most of their lives on the Continent, moving between Paris, Trieste and Zurich. The couple had two children, a son Giorgio and a daughter Lucia. Realising that without a marriage certificate there could be inheritance complications for their children in the future, the couple decided to get married quietly at a London registry office in 1931. However, an eagle-eyed journalist spotted their names on the lists of the registry office and their wedding was made public.

On return trips to Ireland, Joyce and Nora visited Galway and her family at Bowling Green. He was particularly fond of Nora's mother, to whom he wrote regularly. Joyce also had correspondence with Nora's uncle, Michael Healy, to whom he sent a first edition of each of his books.

The Joyces were obviously a passionate couple as is evident from their letters to each other. One of these, somewhat erotic in content, sold at Sotheby's in London for £240,000 in 2004.

Nora remained in Zurich after Joyce died in 1941, surviving him by ten years. Her mother lived at Bowling Green until her death in 1939.

Sir Valentine Blake, Landowner (1780–1847)
The Blakes were one of the Tribes of Galway. They had lands on the shore of the River Corrib at Menlo. One of the most colourful members of that family was Sir Valentine Blake, the 12th Baronet Blake of Galway. Unfortunately for him, he was constantly in debt but he had a number of devious ways of avoiding the bailiffs. Under the laws of the day, bailiffs were not allowed to serve writs on debtors on a Sunday. Knowing this, Sir Valentine would only venture into the city on a Sunday, remaining on his estate for the rest of the week. He soon became known as 'Sunday Boy Blake'. In 1812 he sought election to the House of Commons, as this would give him immunity to writs served by his debtors. However, he needed to canvas for votes. This he did from a boat on the river, as he knew that he could not be served a writ while on water. He was elected and served as an MP for Galway Borough from 1812 to 1820.

A supporter of Catholic Emancipation, it was Sir Valentine Blake who encouraged Daniel O'Connell to put himself forward for election to Parliament in Co. Clare in 1828. O'Connell was elected and through his efforts the Catholic Emancipation Act was passed the following year.

Thomas H. Burke, Civil Servant (1829–1882)

Thomas Henry Burke was born at Waterslade House in Tuam. In 1869 he was appointed Permanent Under-secretary for Ireland, making him the most senior civil servant in Ireland during the difficult period of the Land War.

On the evening of 6 May 1882, he was walking through Dublin's Phoenix Park with the new Chief Secretary for Ireland, Lord Frederick Cavendish. The Chief Secretary had only just arrived in Ireland and they were walking to his lodgings at Deerfield (today the Residence of the US Ambassador to Ireland) when they were set upon by four men with knives. Both men were killed in what became known as the 'Phoenix Park Murders'. It is thought that Burke was the target of the attack as he had made some unpopular decisions during his time as Under-secretary. A group calling themselves 'The Invincibles' claimed responsibility. Seven were later captured; one turned state's evidence and the other six were hanged.

Robert Burke O'Hara, Explorer (1821–1861)

Robert Burke O'Hara was born at St Clerans House, near Craughwell, in 1821. He served in the British Army and later went to Australia, where he joined the police force. In 1860 he was appointed leader of the Victorian Exploring Expedition. The plan was to cross Australia from south to north going from Melbourne to the Gulf of Carpentaria, taking in territories where no white man had ever ventured.

With Burke as their leader and William John Willis (an English surveyor and explorer) as his second in command, a team of nineteen men with horses and camels left Melbourne on 20 August 1860. Leaving most of the team at a base camp at Cooper's Creek in Queensland, Burke, Willis and two others, Charles Gray and John King, finally reached the estuary of the Flinders River on the north coast of Australia on 11 February 1861.

During their return trek to their base camp, Gray died. Burke, Willis and King finally reached the camp on 21 April, only to find it deserted. The base camp party had left just nine hours earlier. Weakened and debilitated, they stayed at the camp, where Burke and Willis died within days of each other. With the help of Aboriginals, King eventually made it back to Melbourne, the only member of the team of nineteen to complete the expedition.

In 1863, the remains of Burke, Willis and King were brought to Melbourne for a state funeral and they were buried in Melbourne General Cemetery. Burketown, the Burke River and O'Hara's Gap in Queensland were named after Robert Burke O'Hara.

Elizabeth 'Daisy' Burke Plunkett, Lady Fingall, Aristocrat (1866–1944)

Lady Fingall's book *Seventy Years Young*, published in 1937, is an account of the twilight years of the landed gentry in Ireland. Daisy – her mother thought that her face was like a wild flower – was born and brought up at Danesfield House, outside Moycullen on the edge of Connemara. Her father George Burke was a magistrate for the region.

She was presented as a debutante at Dublin Castle in 1883, where she met Arthur James Fingall, Earl of Fingall and State Stewart for the Lord Lieutenant of Ireland. He had recently inherited his title and Killeen Castle in Co. Meath. They were soon married and her life became a whirl of travel, dinner parties and fox hunting.

Daisy Fingall knew everybody from politicians and writers to royalty and soldiers. She met Charles Stewart Parnell and was enchanted by his smile. Sir Hugh Lane helped her to refurbish Killeen Castle. She was a regular correspondent of Field Marshal Douglas Haig. She chaperoned Constance Gore Booth during her debutante season. Lady Fingall was also a favourite dinner guest of King Edward VII.

One of her closest friends was Horace Plunkett, founder of the agricultural cooperative movement. She regularly hosted dinners for him at his Dublin home, Kilteragh House. George Bernard Shaw and his wife, the painter Sir John Lavery and his wife Hazel, and Michael Collins attended one such dinner in 1922. A week later, Collins was killed in Co. Cork.

In 1912 Daisy Fingall was involved in the founding of the United Irishwomen, later the Irish Countrywomen's Association. She is buried at Killeen, Co. Meath.

Éamonn Ceannt, Signatory of 1916 Proclamation (1881–1916)
Edmund Kent was born in the police barracks in the village of Ballymoe, on the Galway-Roscommon border in 1881. His father was a policeman with the Royal Irish Constabulary (RIC). The family moved to Ardee, Co. Louth and later to Dublin, where Edmund completed his education with the Christian Brothers. On leaving school, he got a clerical position with Dublin Corporation.

In the early 1900s Ireland was in the throes of the Celtic Revival and Edmund did not escape its influences. Passionate about the Irish language, he joined the Gaelic League and changed his name to the Irish version. Éamonn Ceannt was a talented musician, and became involved in reviving traditional Irish music, setting up the Dublin Piper's Club with another Galway man, Edward Martyn. In 1908 he travelled to Rome and played the uilleann pipes for Pope Pius X.

That was also the year he joined Sinn Féin. He was soon admitted to the Irish Republican Brotherhood (IRB) and was involved in setting up the Irish Volunteers. By 1914 he was at the heart of the IRB movement and, with Padraig Pearse and Joseph Plunkett, made up the IRB Military Committee, tasked with planning an insurrection: the Easter Rising of 1916.

A signatory of the Proclamation of the Irish Republic, Ceannt led the 4th Battalion of the Irish Volunteers during the Easter Rising and held the South Dublin Union (today St James's Hospital) to the very end of Easter week.

He was sentenced to death for his part in the Rising and executed in Kilmainham Jail on 8 May 1916.

The railway station in Galway city is named after him.

Count Patrick D'Arcy, Scientist and Soldier (1725–1779)
Count Patrick D'Arcy was truly a son of the 'Tribes of Galway'. His mother was a Lynch, his maternal grandmother was a Blake and his aunt married a Martin. He was born at Kiltullagh House in East Galway in 1725, and as Catholics and Jacobite supporters, the family felt the full effects of the Penal Laws, which prohibited Catholics from having their children educated.

Patrick was sent to France, travelling with his uncle, a wine merchant. There he lived with another D'Arcy relative in Paris.

An intelligent boy, he began studying mathematics at the age of 14 and presented papers to the Académie Royale des Sciences at 17. In 1749 he became a member of the Académie and would later become a director.

Over his lifetime he studied mathematics, dynamics, electricity, astronomy and the science of artillery. He contributed to a theory on angular momentum and invented a device which measured the recoil of a canon. He was created a count by the French king in recognition of his work

Count D'Arcy saw combat with the French army during the Austrian Wars of Succession and the Seven Years' War. Following in his family's footsteps as a Jacobite, he was captured by the English en route to Scotland to help with Bonnie Prince Charlie's rebellion in 1745, and spent some time in the Tower of London.

In 1777 he married his 16-year-old niece, Jane D'Arcy. He died of cholera two years later and is buried in Paris. His wife later became a lady-in-waiting to Queen Marie-Antoinette, but returned to Ireland before the French Revolution.

Honora De Burgo, Wife of Patrick Sarsfield (1675–1698)
Honora was the daughter of the 7th Earl of Clanricarde and was born at the family's ancestral home of Portumna Castle. At the age of 15 she married Patrick Sarsfield, 1st Earl of Lucan, a title bestowed upon him by King James II. Sarsfield led the Jacobite cause in Ireland during the War of the Two Kings. He fought at the Battle of the Boyne in 1690, the Battle of Aughrim in 1691 and eventually signed the Treaty of Limerick with General Ginkel in 1691. When King William III reneged on that treaty and pursued Jacobites who had fought against him, many fled Ireland. This 'Flight of the Wild Geese' saw Irish soldiers fleeing to France. Sarsfield and his young wife were 'wild geese'. In France the Jacobites, including Sarsfied, joined the French in fighting the Nine Years' War. He was killed at the Battle of Landen in 1693, leaving Honora and their young son almost destitute. She was saved by the Duke of Berwick, the illegitimate son of King James II whom she had once met at Portumna Castle. They fell in love and were married. She died of consumption in France in 1698.

Richard 'Dick' Dowling, Confederate Soldier (c. 1838–1867)
Richard Dowling was born in Milltown in 1838. His family emigrated to America around 1846, eventually settling in Houston, Texas. Dick Dowling had a number of different careers. He started as a saloon owner, then became a banker before raising an army known as the Davis Guards when the American Civil War broke out. In 1863 he was tasked with defending the Sabine Pass between Texas and Louisiana from the Union Army. With just forty-seven men and six cannons, they captured two Union gunboats and 350 prisoners without suffering any casualties themselves.

He died of yellow fever in 1867. Regarded as a hero in the southern states, in 1905 a statute of him was erected in Houston.

Father Edward Flanagan, Founder of Boys Town (1886–1948)
Although born on the Roscommon side of the River Suck at Ballymoe, Co. Galway, the town claims him as a famous son and has erected a statue of him. He was ordained into the priesthood in 1912 and later settled in Omaha, Nebraska in America, where he set up a home for wayward boys which became known as 'Boys Town'. In his opinion there was no such thing as a bad boy; he believed delinquents could be rehabilitated with education. One day Fr Flanagan offered help to a young boy carrying his disabled brother. The boy replied, 'He ain't heavy, he's my brother', which became the motto for Boys Town.

His success in dealing with wayward boys became widely known when a film, *Boys Town*, starring Spencer Tracy and Mickey Rooney, and loosely based on Fr Flanagan's life, was released in 1938. Tracy won an Oscar for his role. The Academy also sent a statuette to Fr Flanagan.

After the Second World War, Harry S. Truman, President of the United States, asked Fr Flanagan to visit Asia and Europe to assess what could be done for the thousands of children who had been displaced and neglected as a result of the war. In 1946 he visited his family in Ireland. He died in Berlin and is buried in Boys Town.

Sir Peter Freyer, Pioneering Surgeon (1851–1921)
Born near Clifden, Peter Freyer was educated at Galway Grammar School and then at Queen's College, Galway (now National University of Ireland Galway, NUIG), first taking a

science degree and then training to become a doctor. He left Ireland to join the Indian Medical Service, where his surgical speciality was removing gallstones and bladder stones. After successfully operating on the Rajah of Rampar to remove a bladder stone, it is said that the grateful Rajah gifted Dr Freyer a small fortune, thought to be £10,000. On returning to London he worked at St Peter's Hospital, where he developed a technique to remove enlarged prostates. He carried out the first prostatectomy in 1900 and was later knighted for his services to medicine. The procedure he used became the standard surgical treatment for an enlarged prostate for the next fifty years, until another Irish doctor, Terence Millin, developed a new procedure in the 1950s. Sir Peter Freyer is buried in Clifden and a lecture and a symposium are held at NUIG in his memory.

Patrick Sarsfield Gilmore, Musician (1829–1892)

Called the 'Father of the American Concert Band' by composer John Philip Sousa, Patrick Sarsfield was born in humble surroundings in Ballygar. He joined the local fife and drum band at an early age and later learnt the trumpet in Athlone. He emigrated to America in 1848, eventually settling in Salem, Massachusetts, where he played at the inauguration of President James Buchanan as a member of the Salem Brigade Band.

During the American Civil War he trained military bands for the Union Army and was inspired to write the song for which he is famous: 'When Johnny Comes Marching Home'. President Abraham Lincoln asked him to organise and perform at a celebratory concert in New Orleans at the end of the war. Encouraged by its success, he soon became involved in organising further concerts and festivals. He moved to New York to create a band especially for these events.

Among the events he directed were the American national centennial celebrations in Philadelphia in 1876. He and his band toured Europe in 1878. They played at the dedication of the Statue of Liberty in 1886 and at the first celebration of New Year's Eve in New York's Times Square in 1891.

Patrick Sarsfield never forgot his Irish roots and was a supporter of Charles Stewart Parnell and the Home Rule movement, and often raised funds for Irish causes at his concerts.

He died in New York in 1892 and is buried there in the Old Cavalry Cemetery.

Father Michael Griffin (1892–1920)

In Galway, the road that leads from the Wolfe Tone Bridge to the Salthill Road has, since 1937, been called 'Fr Griffin Road' after a young priest who had only served in the city for two years before being killed by the Crown Forces during the War of Independence in 1920.

Fr Griffin was born in the village of Gurteen, near Athenry in 1892. He was educated at Garbally College in Ballinasloe and then trained at the seminary in Maynooth to become a priest for the diocese of Clonfert. Following his ordination he was seconded to the Diocese of Galway, working first in Ennistymon, Co. Clare and then in the parish of Barna and Furbo. He lived at Montpellier Terrace in Galway and it was from here that he disappeared on the night of 14 November 1920. That night three men called to the house and, according to the housekeeper, Fr Griffin dressed and left with them. It was thought that he may have gone on a sick call, but he had not brought the necessary prayer book and oils.

His body was found buried in a bog on the road between Moycullen and Barna on 20 November 1920. He had been shot through the head. The murder of a man of the cloth, probably by the Black and Tans, caused outrage around the country. While Fr Griffin had a known interest in nationalist politics and was a strong supporter of the Irish language, he was not vocal in his political ideas. It is generally believed that he was executed in retaliation for the murder of P.W. Joyce by the Connemara East Brigade of the Irish Volunteers. Joyce, a national school teacher from Barna, was a Crown Forces informer.

Fr Griffin's funeral brought Galway to a standstill. He is buried in the grounds of St Brendan's Cathedral, Loughrea, as he was a priest of the Clonfert diocese. A monument was erected over his grave.

Richard Kirwan, Scientist and Eccentric (1733–1812)

Richard Kirwan was born at Cloughballymore Castle near Kinvara, but grew up at the Kirwan family estate of Cregg Castle,

Corrandulla. As the second son, and thus not in line to inherit the family fortune, his family planned for him to enter the priesthood and sent him to France. At Poitiers he developed a keen interest in chemistry, abandoned the Jesuits and, in a further act of rebellion, later converted to Protestantism.

When his brother was killed in a duel in 1755, Richard inherited the family fortune. He returned to Galway and married Anne Blake of Menlo Castle.

He dedicated his life to the sciences, even building a laboratory at Cregg Castle. He largely studied mineralogy and meteorology, but it is his work in the field of chemistry for which he is best known. Kirwan was a supporter of the phlogiston theory. He believed that a gas, phlogiston, was emitted when a substance combusted. On reading Kirwan's paper on the subject, the French chemist Antoine Lavoisier was prompted to put forward his theory that combustion was caused by taking a gas from the air, and not emitting one. Lavoisier called this gas oxygen. Kirwan eventually abandoned his theory in favour of Lavoisier's.

Kirwan was quite an eccentric. He kept a pet eagle and a pack of wolfhounds. He had an obsessive fear of catching a cold, and so always wore a coat, hat and scarves indoors and before he went out he would stand in front of a fire to absorb as much heat as possible. He used the necessity of always wearing a hat as an excuse for never entering a church. Richard Kirwan died at the age of 79, from a cold.

Richard Martin, Landowner and Politician (1754–1834)

Richard Martin is one of Galway's most colourful historical characters. He was a great-grandson of another Richard Martin, who had been given the nickname 'Nimble Dick' after persuading King William III to allow him to keep the family estates in Connemara after the War of the Two Kings. Like his great-grandfather, Richard Martin would acquire not one, but two nicknames.

The first of these, 'Hair Trigger Dick', he earned because he fought over 100 duels during his life. If he saw someone being cruel to an animal, he would challenge them to a duel, which led to his second nickname, 'Humanity Dick'. Impressed by Martin's love of animals, King George IV gave him the latter.

When asked why he preferred animals to people, Humanity Dick once said, 'Did you ever see an ox with a pistol?'

At the age of 22 he won a seat in the Irish Parliament and after the Act of Union he represented Galway in the House of Commons until 1826. His compassion for animals led to the passing of the Martin Act of 1822, making it a criminal offence to mistreat animals. Often ridiculed for his preference for animals over people, after a meeting in a coffee shop with like-minded souls in London in 1824, he founded the Royal Society for the Prevention of Cruelty to Animals.

He inherited a vast estate of 200,000 acres in Connemara and lived mainly at Ballynahinch Castle. He once boasted to his friend King George IV that the Long Walk at Windsor Castle was nothing compared to the 40-mile-long avenue of his estate, which went from the door of Ballynahinch to Galway city. He was extravagant, spending money on animal welfare projects and his estate. But he neglected to collect rents, which made him popular with his tenants but meant that he was in considerable debt by the 1820s. As a Member of Parliament, however, he was immune from prosecution for debt.

In 1826 he lost this privilege when he lost his parliamentary seat. An investigation into his bid for re-election found that many of his tenants had voted numerous times. Now open to prosecution from his debtors, Humanity Dick fled Ireland, never to return. He moved to France and lived out his last days in Boulogne-sur-Mer.

Farrell Pelly, Actor (1891–1963)

Pelly was born in Galway. He joined the Abbey Theatre in 1911 and worked as an actor and a stage manager until 1915. He is best known for appearances in Hollywood films in the latter years of his life. His most famous role was as Paddy Scanlon in Walt Disney's *Darby O'Gill and the Little People*, which was released in 1959. He also had roles in such notable films as *The Iceman Cometh* (1960) and *Arsenic and Old Lace* (1962). He died in New York in 1963.

Alice Perry, Civil Engineer (1885–1969)

Alice Perry was born in Wellpark. She began studying at Queen's College, Galway in 1902, graduating in 1906 with a first-class honours degree in civil engineering. She was the first woman in Ireland or Great Britain to be awarded an engineering degree. Her father was a co-founder of the Galway Electric Light Company. When he died in 1906 he was the County Surveyor. Alice filled the role temporarily, but was not given the job. She emigrated to Glasgow, where she married. Her husband was killed during the First World War. She retired from engineering in 1921 and dedicated her life to writing poetry.

In March 2017 the new engineering building at NUIG became the Alice Perry Engineering Building.

Philip Treacy Millner (b.1967)

Philip Treacy comes from the town of Ahascragh. He studied at the National College of Art and Design in Dublin before heading for the bright lights of London, where he began working as a milliner. His hats have been worn at royal weddings and film premieres.

PEOPLE WITH GALWAY CONNECTIONS

Lady Ampthill, Christabel Russell (1896–1976)

Lady Ampthill, who lived at Dunguaire Castle in Kinvara, was embroiled in a famous divorce case in London during the 1920s. In 1918 she had married John Russell, heir to Lord Ampthill. In 1921 Christabel became pregnant, but her husband sued for divorce, claiming that since their marriage had never been consummated, the child could not be his. Doctors brought in to argue for Christabel famously declared that she was indeed pregnant, but that she was also a virgin. She was nonetheless found guilty of adultery, and her husband granted a divorce. She appealed this decision, lost, and then referred the matter to the House of Lords. In 1924, the House of Lords rescinded the divorce using the argument that granting the divorce would result in her son being declared illegitimate. It was the scandal of the age.

Christabel eventually agreed to divorce her husband in 1937. In 1954, she bought Dunguaire Castle, refurbished it and lived out the rest of her days riding side-saddle with the Galway Blazers. She died in 1976 as a result of a hunting accident.

Edward Carson, Unionist Politician (1854–1935)

The father of Irish Unionism has two connections with Galway. Carson's mother was Isabella Lambert of Castle Ellen near Athenry. He spent many of his childhood summers there and learnt how to play hurling, not a sport typically associated with the Unionist community he would later come to lead.

In 1879 he met and married Annette Kirwan in Dublin. She was the daughter of a retired RIC Inspector, H. Persse Kirwan, formerly of Ballinasloe. Annette died in 1913 and Carson remarried to a Yorkshire lady, Ruby Frewen, in 1914.

Hubert George de Burgh Canning, 15th Earl of Clanricade (1832–1916)

In 1867 Lord Dunkellin, the highly regarded heir to the Clanricarde estates, died. Younger brother Hubert was next in line to inherit 57,000 acres of land and Portumna Castle.

He worked in the British diplomatic service. During his time there, one French diplomat he encountered could not be persuaded that Hubert was the son of an aristocrat, due to his unkempt appearance.

In 1874 Hubert became the fifteenth earl on the death of his father. He soon became that most despised breed of landlord: the absentee. It is said that the only time he set foot on the Clanricarde estate was to attend his father's funeral. The 1,900 tenants of the estate yielded him an annual income of £24,000. He lived in London, was frugal with his money and never married. He took his late brother's seat in Parliament but resigned it in 1871, as he was opposed to the Land Act of that year, which aimed to improve the lot of Irish tenant farmers. In 1882 Lord Clanricarde's agent, John Henry Blake, was shot dead on his way to church in Loughrea. But worse was to come. In August 1886 an incident on the Clanricarde estate made headlines around the world.

Thomas Saunders was the tenant of a 40-acre farm on the Clanricarde estate, near Woodford. He had made improvements to the farm, and under new rules was entitled to a reduction in his rent. As the earl refused to implement the new rules, by way of protest, Saunders refused to pay rent and was in arrears. He was to be evicted. A huge crowd gathered to oppose the eviction. Seven hundred policemen and 200 soldiers were dispatched to Woodford to deal with the situation. The police gained access to the barricaded cottage through the roof, and arrested Saunders and twenty-one others who were in the cottage with him. They were all sentenced to prison terms of between twelve and eighteen months. One of those arrested, Thomas Larkin, died while in prison in Kilkenny. It is said that 20,000 people attended his funeral.

This episode led to the Earl of Clanricarde becoming the most hated landlord in Ireland and gained him the title 'Lord Clan Rack Rent'. In 1915 the Congested District Board bought the Clanricarde estate. Lord Clanricarde died the following year. As he had never married he had no direct heir and his wealth of £2,500,000 went to his grand-nephew Henry Lascelles, later Lord Harwood.

Oliver St John Gogarty (1878–1957)

Oliver St John Gogarty was a surgeon, a poet and an Irish Nationalist.

His mother was Margaret Oliver from Eyre Square in Galway. He was born and educated in Dublin, and qualified as an ear, nose and throat surgeon. He furthered his Galway connections by marrying Martha Duane of Moyard in Connemara.

In 1917 they bought Renvyle House in Connemara. They regularly travelled from Dublin, usually in Gogarty's yellow Rolls-Royce, and entertained well-known guests. Among his literary friends was W.B. Yeats. Yeats and his new bride, George Hyde-Lees, spent their honeymoon at Renvyle in 1917. James Joyce, another of Gogarty's literary friends, depicted him as the colourful Buck Milligan in *Ulysses*.

Gogarty was also friendly with important political figures such as Arthur Griffiths and Michael Collins. He supported Collins in his pro-Treaty position and was appointed a Senator in the new Irish Free State. When Civil War erupted, he sided with Collins. He performed Collins's autopsy after he was killed in August 1922.

Gogarty became a target for the anti-Treaty forces. In 1923 they burnt Renvyle House to the ground, and he escaped an attempted kidnapping in Dublin that same year by jumping into the River Liffey. He and Martha later rebuilt Renvyle and opened it as a hotel.

In a further adventure, Gogarty escaped a plane crash in Connemara in 1928. In the 1920s he bought Dunguaire Castle, near Kinvara, for £90, hoping that the royalties from his book *As I Was Going Down Sackville Street* would pay for the refurbishment. He only managed to pay to reroof the castle, because he was sued for libelling a jeweller in his book and was fined £800.

He died in New York, where he had spent the last ten years of his life writing and giving lecture tours, while his wife remained at home in Renvyle House.

Sir William Gregory, Landowner and Politician (1817–1892)

Born in Dublin Castle, where his grandfather was the Under-Secretary to the Lord Lieutenant, Sir William's ancestral home was Coole Park near Gort. He was 24 before he visited Coole Park for the first time.

He became a Member of Parliament for Dublin in 1842. His best-known contribution to Parliament is 'The Gregory Clause', which was added to the Poor Relief Extension Act of 1847. The Gregory Clause stipulated that only tenants with a holding of a quarter-acre or less could claim poor relief. As the landlords were responsible for funding the relief effort, it was included for their benefit, in the hope of reducing the number of tenants who could claim relief, even though those with larger holdings were equally in need of assistance. The Archbishop of Tuam, Dr McHale, thereafter called him 'Quarter Acre' Gregory.

Gregory's father died that year after contracting 'famine fever' while helping his tenants. When he inherited the Coole Park estate, Sir William proved himself a conscientious landlord and never evicted a tenant.

Between 1872 and 1877 he served as the fourteenth Governor of British Ceylon (now Sri Lanka). The Prince of Wales knighted him for his work there. Today there is a Gregory's Road and a statue of Sir Gregory outside the National Museum in Colombo.

He had a keen interest in the arts, and was appointed a trustee of the National Gallery of Ireland in 1867. He paid for the restoration of the Round Tower at Kilmacdugh in 1879.

His first wife, Elizabeth Temple Bowdoin, died in 1873. In 1880 he married 28-year-old Augusta Persse from the neighbouring Roxborough House estate. She is better known as Lady Gregory, co-founder of the Abbey Theatre. They had one son, Robert.

Gregory died in London but his remains were brought back to Co. Galway and he was interred in the family vault behind Kiltartan church.

William Joyce, 'Lord Haw-Haw' (1906–1946)

Better known as 'Lord Haw-Haw', William Joyce was hanged for high treason in 1946 at Wandsworth Prison in London. During the Second World War he had made radio broadcasts in English promoting Nazism. His family lived in Galway between 1909 and 1921 and because of this connection to the city, his daughter requested that he be buried in Galway. In 1976 his remains were reinterred at the New Cemetery in Bohermore.

Michael Morris, 3rd Baron Killanin (1914–1999)

A descendant of the Morris Tribe, Michael Morris was born in London in 1914, the year that his father, George Henry Morris, died serving with the Irish Guards on the battlefields of France. He was educated at Eton College, the Sorbonne in Paris and Magdalen College in Cambridge. At the age of 13 he became 3rd Baron Killanin, inheriting the title from his uncle, Martin Henry Fitzpatrick Morris, the 2nd Baron Killanin, who had died leaving no direct heir.

Serving in the British army during the Second World War, Lord Killanin was involved in the D-Day landings on the Normandy coast in 1944 and was later honoured with an MBE for his military service.

In 1945 he married Sheila Cathcart Dunlop after meeting her at the Galway Races. She had grown up in Oughterard, the daughter of a rector, and like her husband had been awarded an MBE, for her work at Bletchley Park during the Second World War. She would later serve as President of the Irish Society for the Prevention of Cruelty to Children.

After the war Lord Killanin worked in film production. He worked on John Ford's *The Quiet Man*. He co-wrote *The Shell Guide to Ireland*, was Chairman of the Galway Race Committee and served on the committee of the Galway Archaeological and Historical Society for many years.

However, Lord Killanin is best known for his presidency of the International Olympic Committee between 1972 and 1980, the period which saw a hostage situation at the Munich Games in 1972 and boycotts of the Moscow Games in 1980. He served two four-year terms on the Committee. He was a talented diplomat and well-respected internationally. The family seat was at Spiddal House, but it was sold in the 1960s. Lord Killanin died in 1999 and is buried in the Morris family vault in the New Cemetery, Bohermore in Galway.

Sir Oswald Mosley, Politician and Leader of the British Union of Fascists (1896–1980)

Sir Oswald Mosley founded the British Union of Fascists in 1932. When the Second World War broke out, because of his Nazi sympathies, both he and his wife Diana Guinness (*née* Mitford) were sent to Holloway Prison. They were released in 1943 and placed under house arrest until the end of the war.

In 1951 they decided to move to Ireland. They bought Clonfert House, the old Bishops Palace close to Clonfert Cathedral, renovated it and divided their time between Co. Galway and France. However, in 1954 a beam close to a chimney caught fire and the house was burnt to the ground. They left Co. Galway and settled permanently in France.

Padraig Pearse, Revolutionary and Political Writer (1879–1916)

The leader of the 1916 Easter Rising first visited Connemara in 1903. He came to Rosmuc as an examiner for the Irish-language organisation the Gaelic League. He was so taken with Connemara that he bought a plot of land and built a small cottage, even opting to put a thatched roof on it in the traditional style.

Pearse would spend his summers here writing and improving his Irish by spending time in the mud-walled thatched cabins of the locals, listening to their stories and learning their language. He was also a regular visitor to the Aran Islands. When he founded an Irish school in Rathfarnam in Dublin, he named it after the patron saint of Aran, St Enda.

As editor of *An Claidheamh Soluis*, a bilingual nationalist newspaper, he wrote political articles in English and Irish. The most famous of his writings is the speech he delivered at the graveside of the Fenian Jeramiah O'Donovan Rossa in 1915. He wrote the speech while staying in Rosmuc.

After Pearse was executed in 1916 for his part in the Easter Rising, the cottage in Rosmuc passed to his mother. It was burnt down in 1921 by the Black and Tans. Pearse's cottage has since been restored and today is a national monument.

Grace O'Malley, Pirate Queen of the West (c. 1530–1603)

While Grace O'Malley was not from Galway, the Galway families of the O'Flahertys, Joyces and Burkes feature in her story. She was the daughter of Dubhdarra O'Malley, a pirate who operated around Clew Bay in the mid-sixteenth century. His fleet of ships controlled the fishing rights of that coastline and Grace learnt her trade from him.

At the age of 16 she married Dónal O'Flatherty, of Connemara, and lived at Bunowen and Ballynahinch. Dónal was murdered by the Joyces of Connemara and under the Gaelic Brehon Laws she became the leader of the O'Flatherty clan. She then had unhindered pirating control of the coast from Clew Bay to Galway city.

Her second husband was Richard Burke. She divorced him and continued to captain the fleet of pirate ships, which by now were targeting the lucrative trade ships coming in and out of Galway.

When Queen Elizabeth I turned her attentions to subduing Connacht, Grace O'Malley became a thorn in her side. In 1584, Sir Richard Bingham was made Governor of Connacht and was determined to put a stop to Grace and her pirates. By 1593, her lands had been confiscated, she had fled to Ulster and her son Tibbot was arrested. Hiring a ship, she sailed to London determined to plead for her son's life face to face with the Queen of England.

They met at Greenwich Palace in September 1593. The Pirate Queen and the English Queen conversed in Latin, the only language they had in common, and somehow Grace came away with her lands returned and her son released. This fiery Irish woman clearly made an impression on Elizabeth I. However, Grace and Bingham remained firm enemies and their feud only ended when he returned to England in disgrace in 1595.

The Pirate Queen of the West died in 1603, the same year as Queen Elizabeth I.

IN BRIEF

Alexander Anderson (1858–1936) was from Coleraine, Co. Derry and studied engineering at Queen's University, Galway. He graduated in 1881 and is credited with identifying the existence of 'black holes'.

Michael D. Higgins (b.1941), the current President of Ireland, is a graduate of University College Galway, where he has also lectured in sociology and politics.

Martin Sheen (b.1940) is best known for his role as Jed Bartlett in the television series *The West Wing*. His mother, Mary Ann Phelan, came from Terryglass in Co. Tipperary. In 2006 he enrolled at NUIG, where he took classes in English literature, philosophy and oceanography.

J.R.R. Tolkien (1892–1973), author of *The Lord of The Rings*, worked as an external examiner at University College Galway in 1949.

Che Guevara (1928–1967), the Argentine revolutionary, was the grandson of Anna Lynch from Galway.

5

THE NATURAL HISTORY OF GALWAY

Galway is the second largest county in Ireland, after Cork. It is a county of contrasts. Lough Corrib, the largest lake in the Republic of Ireland, forms a natural divide between two very different landscapes. To the west is the unspoilt wilderness of Connemara sweeping towards the Atlantic Ocean, with the mountain ranges of the Twelve Bens and the Mamturks, lakes and bog land. To the east is a low-lying limestone plateau dotted with disappearing lakes and bordered to the south by the low hills of the Slieve Aughty range.

The Aran Islands provide Co. Galway with a third unique landscape, as they are a continuation of the barren landscape of the Burren of Co. Clare.

Co. Galway has borders with five other counties. From Kinvara on the coast and through Slieve Aughty, Galway borders Co. Clare. The border continues through the centre of Lough Derg, which separates Galway from Co. Tipperary. The Shannon is the natural border between Galway and Co. Offaly. The River Suck, a tributary of the Shannon, forms a natural border with Co. Roscommon as far north as Ballymoe, where the borders of Galway and Mayo meet, continuing to the coastline and Killary Harbour.

THE COAST AND ISLANDS

Galway has 300km (187 miles) of Atlantic coastline. Beginning at Kinvara in the south, winding its way through Galway city and out along the undulating coast of Connemara, it takes in award-winning beaches and rugged islands.

Killary Harbour

Killary Harbour in the north of the county is Ireland's only fjord. Glacial erosion caused by the thawing ice from the last ice age carved a valley between the Mweelrea Mountains on the Mayo side of the harbour and the foothills of the Maamturks on the Galway side. This water-filled valley is fed by the River Erriff and curves its way past the village of Leenane and out into the Atlantic. The mouth of the harbour is 14km (9 miles) from the Aasleagh Falls, site of a fight scene in the 1990 film *The Field*. Killary Harbour is deepest down its centre, where at points it is 45m (148ft) deep. Since the 1980s, blue mussels have been farmed there. They attach themselves to the ropes suspended from the barrels bobbing on the waters of the harbour.

Beaches of Connemara

Before Irish people started holidaying in sunny climes, they went to seaside resorts in Ireland. One of the best known was Galway's Salthill. Many of the hotels are long gone and few of the amusement arcades remain, but today the Prom bustles with dog walkers and joggers.

The extensive coastline of Co. Galway offers some of the most beautiful and unspoilt beaches in Ireland. Two miles west of Galway city is the beautiful Silver Strand at Barna. In Connemara the 1-mile sweep of beach at Dog's Bay is a well-kept secret. Washed by the clear water of the Atlantic Ocean, these white sandy beaches have won environmental awards.

In 2010 a winter storm washed away stone and sand from a beach near Spiddal, revealing the stumps of an extensive oak, pine and birch forest thought to be 7,500 years old.

Trá an Dóilin near Carraroe is not like the other beaches of Co. Galway. Instead of white sand, the beach is made up of little fragments of a white, chalky deposit that resembles coral.

However, there are no coral reefs in Galway Bay. William McAlla (1814–1849), a schoolmaster from Roundstone, realised that the deposit was a form of plant life. Naturalists have since identified the plants as *Lithothamnium coralloide* and *Phymatolithon calcareum*, more commonly referred to as coral algae or maerl. They are a type of seaweed that are not attached to the seabed, are slow growing and found in deep waters. The frond of the plant develops a calcified outer layer to protect it from feeding fish. Living plants are red, but when they die and are washed ashore they become white and chalky.

Seaweed

There are approximately 560 different types of seaweed on the Irish shoreline. In a region short on natural resources, the coastal dwellers found multiple uses for this abundant gift of the sea.

On the Aran Islands and other coastal areas of Galway, the thin layer of soil covering the bedrock is not suitable for growing crops. To deepen the soil, islanders carried basket-loads of the larger red-and-black seaweed from the shore to their small fields. By mixing it with sand and manure, they were able to deepen and fertilise the poor soil, enabling them to grow oats, barley and rye. Deepening the soil further made it possible to grow potatoes. These crops did not only provide food: rye straw was used for thatching roofs.

Certain seaweeds are also edible, notably carrageen and dillisk. Carrageen Moss is found in rock pools. It acts as a thickening agent and was cooked in milk to make blancmange. It was also used to treat ailments such as coughs and sore throats. Dillisk was a particularly useful remedy for a hangover.

During the mid to late eighteenth century a more commercial use was found for seaweed. It contains minerals such as calcium, iodine, magnesium, potassium and sodium, and it was found that when burned, these minerals could be extracted from the resulting molten substance. This was known as 'kelp'. It was used in manufacturing soap, glass and gunpowder. Kelp was also used for glazing china and pottery, and for bleaching linen. As the age of industrialisation dawned, demand for kelp grew.

Between May and August, islanders would undertake the backbreaking work of gathering red-and-black seaweed at low tide, cutting it from the rocks with sharp knives. It would then be carried above the high tide line and allowed to dry. In September they would burn it in makeshift kilns lined with stones gathered from the shore to make kelp. Five tonnes of dried seaweed could yield 1 tonne of kelp. By the early 1900s, demand for kelp had fallen as the industries that traditionally used kelp had found cheaper and more efficient ways of sourcing the minerals they needed. But that was not the end of the seaweed story in Galway.

In 1947, the Irish government set up a state-run company, Arramara Teoranta, based in Cill Chiaráin in Connemara. It worked in conjunction with University College, Galway (originally Queen's College, now NUIG) to find new ways of exploiting this abundant natural resource. Today yellow seaweed is harvested and processed in Connemara. It is used to make top soil fertiliser, animal feed and alginates. The latter is used in the cosmetic industry for potions and lotions, as suspensions for medicines and in the food industry as a thickening agent, labelled as E407 or E407b, in products such as ice cream, sauces and even beer.

Oysters

There are 700 acres of oyster beds off the Galway coast at Clarinbridge. Oysters require a combination of fresh and seawater to thrive. At Clarinbridge, the Clarin and Dunkellin rivers converge and meet the sea, creating an ideal environment for oysters. For three years the oyster sits on its bed, filtering up to 190 litres (50 gallons) of fresh water and seawater through its shell every day. The oyster draws in nutrients and vitamins of the sea, making it firm, yet succulent, full of flavour and ready for harvesting.

Our ancient ancestors were partial to oysters: there is evidence of oyster shells in middens, the rubbish tips of prehistoric man. In the nineteenth century, oysters were the food of the poor and were eaten during famine times. This lowly bivalve mollusc is often thought of as an aphrodisiac. That most famous of lovers, Casanova, may have enhanced the oyster's reputation, as he was in the habit of devouring large quantities at a time.

To celebrate this most interesting of bivalves, a festival was organised in Galway in September 1954. September is traditionally the beginning of the oyster season. It is said that oysters should only be eaten in a month containing the letter 'r' because, in the days before refrigeration, the heat of the summer months would spoil them and make them unfit to eat. Over sixty years later, the Galway Oyster Festival attracts 20,000 people to the city on the last weekend of September to enjoy freshly harvested Galway Bay oysters.

The Aran Islands

At the mouth of Galway Bay, three islands rise like grey whales from the sea. The Aran Islands of Inishmore, Inishmaan and Inisheer are just 9.6km(6 miles) from the mainland. Inishmore, the Big Island, is 13.5km (8.5 miles) long and at points no wider than 4km (2.5 miles). St Gregory's Sound separates Inishmore from Inishmaan, the Middle Island, which is 13km (9 miles) in circumference. The Foul Sound is a 3km (2 mile) strait between Inishmaan and Inisheer, the Eastern Island. Inisheer is the smallest, covering an area of 8 square kilometres (5 square miles) and is the island closest to the Co. Clare coastline.

The islands boast a rich heritage of prehistoric and early Christian sites. The legendary Fir Bolg came here after their defeat by the Tuatha Dé Dannan and built the cliff-edge fort at Dun Aengus, the most spectacular of numerous stone forts on the three islands. Saints followed, with St Enda founding a monastery here in AD 490 where he trained other saints, such as St Jarlath of Tuam and St Ciarán of Clonmacnoise.

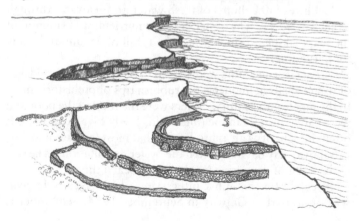

While they lie in the administrative district of Co. Galway, geologically, the Aran Islands are a continuation of the unusual limestone landscape of the Burren in Co. Clare. The thin layer of soil that once covered the bare limestone has been eroded away over the millennia, leaving only about one-tenth of the islands' surface suitable for arable farming. The Aran islanders made the best of the limited resources available to them. With no turf, very few trees and poor soil, the islanders exploited the sea to survive. They fished, using their traditional rowing boat, the *currach*, and they harvested seaweed. Today the islanders welcome 200,000 visitors each year, making tourism the main industry. Visitors travel as foot passengers on ferries from Rossaveal or Doolin in Co. Clare. Once on the islands, they can hire bicycles, rent a local taxi or tour the island in a traditional horse-drawn jaunting car. There is also an air service from Inverin to Inishmore.

The Aran Island climate is moderate, with a mean temperature of 6 degrees in January. Since the soil temperature rarely falls below this, crops and vegetation have a longer growing period than on the colder mainland. Cattle grazed on the islands during the winter months are often brought to the mainland for 'finishing', where they graze on more fertile pastures to fatten them up.

The islands are not lacking in stone. Once scattered across the islands, over the centuries the loose stones were gathered and used to build dry stone walls around cleared fields. The walls provided shelter for crops and animals from the ocean winds.

Prior to the Potato Famine of the 1840s, the islands had a population of 3,500. Today approximately 1,200 people live on the Aran Islands.

Inishbofin
North of the Aran Islands is the smaller inhabited island of Inishbofin. It is 11km (7 miles) off the Galway coast and can be reached by ferry from Cleggan. Legend suggests that Inishbofin, which translates as the 'Island of the White Cow', once floated on the high seas and was not fixed to any point. One day two fog-bound fishermen found the island and took refuge on it. They lit a fire, which fixed the island where it was.

When the fog lifted, the two men saw an old woman driving a white cow to a lake on the island. She struck the cow and it turned to stone. Any reappearance of the cow is said to be a herald of disaster.

St Colman founded a monastery in the early Christian era and in AD 795 Inishbofin was the first place in the west of Ireland to be attacked by the Vikings. The most impressive ruin on the island is a Cromwellian fort which overlooks the harbour, where the boats arrive from Cleggan. The now ruined fort was built in 1656, and was used to hold imprisoned Catholic priests until they could be transported to the West Indies.

In 1841 the island sustained a population of 1,400. Today approximately 160 people live on Inishbofin.

Inishshark

Neighbouring Inishbofin is the much smaller Inishshark. In 1960 the last twenty-three inhabitants were relocated to the mainland along with thirteen cows, twelve dogs, ten donkeys, eight cats, a hundred sheep and lots of hens.

CONNEMARA

The Bogs of Connemara

In 10,000 BC Ireland was covered in ice. When the thaw set in, water levels rose, submerging the land bridges that linked Ireland to Britain and Europe. Vegetation grew on the resulting waterlogged island. Due to a lack of microorganisms and oxygen in these watery plains, the dead vegetation accumulated to form the peat of the bogs.

In Ireland there are two types of bog land: raised bogs and blanket bogs. The raised bogs of the Midlands formed in lake basins. The bogs of Co. Galway and the west of Ireland are mainly blanket bogs. The moisture that creates blanket bogs comes from high levels of rainfall, unlike the raised bogs where the water comes from lakes. Blanket bogs spread out over the poorly drained landscape – like blankets. Connemara and parts of East Galway have a landscape of blanket bogs.

The Bog Bodies

The lack of microorganisms in bog land prevents full decomposition. In 1929 the skeletal remains of a prehistoric man were recovered in a bog on the shores of Lough Derg. Carbon dating revealed that 'Stoneyleigh Man' roamed this part of Galway around 3300 BC. Other bogs have given up more intact remains.

In 1821 the O'Kelly family were turf cutting on their land near Castleblakney when they came across human remains buried in the bog. The body had clearly been in there for a very long time, so they knew it was not a victim of a recent crime. In an era when archaeology was not a priority for land owners, the family reburied the body, only uncovering it when curious visitors wanted to see their grisly find. This exposure to air led to the decomposition of the bog body. In 1829 the Royal Irish Academy took it for preservation. For many years 'Gallagh Man' was the only bog body exhibited in the National Museum of Ireland. Research on him revealed that he probably lived about 300 BC. He was most likely murdered, by strangulation, and was buried naked except for a deerskin cloak draped around his shoulders.

Turf Cutting

The raised hummocks, the pools of water and spongy waterlogged surface of the bog landscape mean that it is of little commercial use. There is little for livestock to graze on and crops cannot be grown in such wet land. Sphagnum moss contributes to retaining the moisture in the bog. Heathers, gorse and the fluffy bog cotton offer a splash of colour to the landscape at different times of the year. Sundew, a carnivorous plant, feasts on the insects that thrive on the bogs. Birds abound, but sightings of the Irish hare, badgers and foxes are rare.

For millennia the bogs provided the only fuel available in rural Ireland. Turf is still cut from them today, in early summer. Using a *slean*, a spade-like implement, sods of turf are cut from the edge of a ridge. In its natural state, this wet turf is not much use as a fuel. 'Footing the turf' involves arranging it in small piles on the top of the bog. This allows air to circulate around the wet sods, drying them out over the summer months. By autumn the turf is dry enough for use, just as the temperatures begin to drop.

In the past, a donkey would have carried the turf in creels or wicker baskets to the farmhouse.

Connemara Ponies

The Connemara pony is the only native horse bred in Ireland. The original ponies are thought to have arrived with the Vikings in the tenth century. In the sixteenth century, Spanish blood was added when Andalusian horses escaped from the wrecked ships of the Spanish Armada. In the eighteenth century, Arabian blood was added to the mix.

This combination has resulted in a sturdy, surefooted pony with great stamina and a gentle temperament. They are usually no more than fourteen hands, have short legs and a strong muscular body. Typically they are grey in colour, although foals are born brown. In the past the ponies were the workhorses of Connemara, pulling ploughs and carrying loads. Their days as workhorses are long gone and today Connemara ponies can be found in showjumping and dressage arenas, trekking the Connemara countryside or gazing over the stone walls of Connemara.

In 1923 the Connemara Pony Society was founded with the aim of preserving the breed. The society began registering animals and started the Connemara Pony Show, which is still held annually in Clifden. By 1926 Connemara ponies were recognised worldwide as an official horse breed.

Connemara Marble

Ireland's only genuine marble is quarried in Connemara. Formed over 500 million years ago, Connemara marble comes mainly in hues of dark and pale green, but can also come in shades of brown and sepia white.

Stone Age man was the first to find a use for the marble, using it for axe heads. It was first quarried commercially in 1822. Richard 'Humanity Dick' Martin of Ballinahinch saw the financial potential in quarrying the serpentine green marble found at Streamstown near Clifden. He gave his good friend King George IV a marble fireplace. However, the lack of roads through Connemara meant that transporting the huge slabs of marble from the quarry to Galway dock took weeks.

The opening of a railway between Galway and Clifden reduced the travel time. In 1895 a New York marble merchant, Robert C. Fisher, bought a quantity of the marble for use in public buildings in America, such as the State Capital building in Harrisburg, Pennsylvania, built in 1906.

Fittingly, the interior of Galway Cathedral boasts the largest expanse of Connemara marble. It has also been used in the interiors of Ceannt Railway Station in Galway and Shannon Airport. Today, while still quarried, it is used mainly for making jewellery and small souvenirs

LAKES, RIVERS AND CANALS

Lough Corrib and the River Corrib
Galway's largest lake takes its name from Orbsen MacAlloid, a Celtic sea god of the Tuatha Dé Dannan. This mystical tribe are said to have defeated the ancient Fir Bolg at Moytura on the shores of the lake. The Fir Bolg fled to the Aran Islands, leaving the Tuatha Dé Dannan to control the wilds of Connemara.

The lake is the second largest in Ireland after Lough Neagh. It is 56km (35 miles) long, between 400m (0.25 miles) and 13km (8 miles) wide, and varies in depth from a few feet in places to 45m (150ft). There are 145 islands on Lough Corrib, where locals hid their illegal poteen stills during the nineteenth century. The lake is drained by the River Corrib which, at 6km (4 miles), is the shortest river in Ireland. The river was originally called the 'Gaillimh', after the daughter of the Celtic chieftain Bressil who fell into the rapid waters and was never seen again. In the nineteenth century the name was changed to the Corrib.

In the twelfth century, the monks of Claregalway Abbey cut a channel through bog land on the south side of Lough Corrib. The Blakes of Menlo, who owned the land, granted the monks permission for the channel, which joined the river, cutting out a long overland route for them to reach the river. To this day the channel is known as the Friar's Cut and is still the main navigation route from Lough Corrib to the river.

The River Corrib may be short, but it is fast, particularly where it flows through Galway city on its way to the sea. In the nineteenth century, up to thirty mills lined the riverbanks, their waterwheels grinding wheat, oats and tree bark.

This fast-flowing part of the river was not navigable. In the 1820s, the Scottish engineer Alexander Nimmo drew up plans for a canal east of the river and through the Woodquay area of the city. He also suggested a canal that would link Lough Mask on the Mayo/Galway border with Lough Corrib, opening the interior of Connemara and Mayo to Galway city.

Funding was not made available for either project until the 1840s. Nimmo's route around the city was rejected in favour of one to the west of the river. The Eglington Canal was opened in 1852. It is 1km (3,200ft) long and has two locks and five swivel bridges. The canal was tolled, collecting £370 in 1880. It was never a commercial success and in 1916 just £1 was collected in tolls. The last boat to use the canal was the *Amo II* in 1954. She belonged to the Guinness family of Ashford Castle and once she had passed through all the swivel bridges were fixed so that the canal could no longer be used.

The Dry Canal at Cong

While Alexander Nimmo's plans for a canal to pass around Galway city were rejected, in 1848 work began on another canal that he had suggested: the Lough Mask Lough Corrib Canal.

The superintending engineer on the project was Samuel Roberts. The digging of the canal and construction of the necessary structures brought much-needed work to an area which had been devastated by the Potato Famine and where there was no industry.

The canal was 7km (4 miles) and was to have three locks, an aqueduct and a series of bridges. All of these stone works were put in place first. It was only when work began on digging the channel through which the water would course its way to Lough Corrib that problems arose. Given the wet climate in the west of Ireland, it was assumed that any rainwater which fell into the newly dug channel would lodge there. Instead it disappeared.

The landscape in that part of Co. Galway is made up of carboniferous limestone, which is very porous. When rainwater comes into contact with this type of stone, it seeps through rather than running on the surface. It erodes the stone and creates subterranean caves and channels.

The water for the new canal kept disappearing and draining underground. Without water, the canal was not fit for purpose and engineers could not find a solution. In 1854, after six years of work, the project was abandoned. Today the stone works, including the canal lock basins, can still be seen in the Cong area.

Turloughs

A feature of the landscape unique to South Galway and parts of Co. Clare is the 'vanishing lake' or 'turlough'. Ten thousand years ago, as Ireland came out of the last ice age, lakes settled in the ice-hollowed carboniferous limestone landscape. The porous nature of the stone meant that streams created to drain the lake did not run on the surface of the landscape. Instead the acidic rainwater seeped underground, eroding the limestone away and making channels and caverns. These channels drained the water into Galway Bay.

When the water table in East Galway rises during the winter, the rainfall fills the lakes, bringing the water level above the drainage channels. A turlough appears. In the summer, when the water table falls, the water seeps away through the underground water channels, leaving a lush green area where there had been a lake.

The town of Turloughmore in East Galway takes its name from its location close to what was the largest turlough in Ireland. A nineteenth-century drainage scheme resulted in the 'disappearing lake' disappearing for good.

Rahasane turlough between Kilcolgan and Clarinbridge is now the largest turlough in the region, covering an area of 250 hectares when fully flooded. It is home to a rare transparent crustacean known as the 'fairy shrimp' (*Tanymasttix stagnalis*), which is not native to Ireland, and was first found in the turlough in 1974.

Also worth mentioning is Caherglasaun turlough near Coole. Linked to Galway Bay 5km (3 miles) away by an underground channel, the water levels of the turlough rise and fall twice daily, lagging behind the high and low tides by a few hours.

In winter when they flood, the turloughs are havens for birds such as mute and whooper swans, and when they drain away in summer, cattle and sheep can be grazed on the nutrient-rich pasture left behind.

EAST GALWAY

Slieve Aughty

Stretching across the south of Co. Galway into Co. Clare are the Slieve Aughty Mountains. The highest point of the range is Maghera in Co. Clare. Maghera is visible for miles, not because of its height – it is only 400m (1,300ft) high – but because of the radio and television broadcast mast on top of it.

According to legend, a princess, Echtghe, of the Tuatha Dé Danann was given the mountain when she married Fergus Lusca Mac Ruidi of the Fir Bolg. She gave the mountain her name, and in return her new husband received two cows as a dowry. The name of the Owendalulagh River, which flows down the side of Slieve Aughty and passes near the village of Derrybrien translates as 'river of the two cows'.

Today the largest wind farm in Ireland is on Slieve Aughty, near Derrybrien. Seventy-one turbines generate enough electricity for 45,000 homes. The development of the wind farm was not without controversy, as it is thought that construction works and deforestation to make way for the turbines led to a massive landslide in the area in October 2003, which polluted local rivers and Lough Cutra, killing 100,000 fish.

Esker Riada

When the thaw of the last ice age began, deposits of sand, gravel and stones lodged in the ice began to move. They accumulated to form sand hills or ridges in the otherwise waterlogged landscape. These sand ridges are known as 'eskers'.

The main accumulation of these gravel deposits was across the narrowest point of Ireland, the route which would later link Dublin and Galway via intervals of solid ridges, which made crossing the boggy Midlands easier. To the ancient Celts, it was

'An Slí Mor' ('the big road'). Later it was known as the Esker Riada. It conveniently intersected with the main north–south travel route, the River Shannon. The natural crossroads of Ireland was therefore on the eastern edge of Connacht. The town of Ahascragh gets its name from Ath Eascrach, the 'Ford of the Esker'.

Dry Stone Walls

There are 400,000km (250,000 miles) of dry stone walls in Ireland and most of them are in East Galway, the Aran Islands and Co. Clare. The craft of dry stone walling has survived for 6,000 years. The Ceide Fields in Co. Mayo were lined with such walls. No tools are required, just a good supply of stones which are fitted and balanced together uncut, in long winding lines of narrow walls. Their intersecting lines give the landscape a patchwork appearance. Most of the walls of East Galway are about 200 years old. In a region where the land is poor, stones were gathered from low-lying areas to clear them for farming. The walls provided shelter for the livestock and crops in the small fields, but were also a way of using the collected stone.

6

THE ARTS IN GALWAY

Galway's reputation as a centre of Irish culture and heritage was recognised in 2016, when Galway won the honour of being the European City of Culture in 2020, beating cities such as Kilkenny, Waterford, Cork and Limerick.

Galway's retention of Ireland's Celtic heritage can be traced back to its remote location on the western seaboard. While Galway city was founded by the Anglo-Normans, the inaccessible areas of Connemara and the Aran Islands remained untouched by outside influences. The Irish language thrived and survived the ravages of the Potato Famine, as did the Celtic culture of storytelling.

Bards such as Antoine Raifteirí were still roaming Galway's countryside in the early 1800s. Later in the century a wave of fervent nationalism spread throughout Ireland and people saw the Irish language as the root of their cultural identity. Scholars came to the Aran Islands to learn the language in its purest form from the native speakers. But in the people of this western Irish-speaking region they also found folklore, traditions and a simple way of life which proved enormously inspirational to a wave of writers in search of new material. Like ripples in a pond, the influences of language and heritage so long preserved on the Aran Islands spread throughout Ireland. The writers of the Celtic Literary Revival of the early twentieth century, which was led by Lady Augusta Gregory from her home at Coole Park, near Gort, drew on the islanders' folklore, legends and way of life for their plays.

The newly independent Ireland provided opportunities for new literature in the Irish language. Fittingly, when the time came for the Irish language to take to the airwaves of radio and television, Co. Galway was the preferred location for studios.

With a cultural heritage spanning from the wandering bards of old to the hub of Irish-language broadcasting, it is small wonder that Galway was chosen as the 2020 European City of Culture.

THE IRISH LANGUAGE

From the Iron Age the language spoken throughout Ireland was the early form of the language which has become known today as Gaelic or Irish. The early Christian monks who followed in the wake of St Patrick put an ornate script on what was until then only a spoken language. Linguistic changes brought by the Anglo Normans did not impact on the native Irish living beyond 'The Pale'. However, English planters were granted lands in Ireland, forcing the native Irish speakers into the remote, inaccessible and less fertile land of the west. The Potato Famine of the nineteenth century was almost the death knell of the language, as it was the native Gaelic speakers who were most affected by the failure of the potato crop. Those who survived kept the language alive. Today Co. Galway is the largest Gaeltacht region in Ireland.

Antoine Raifteirí (c. 1779–1835)
The opening line of Raifteirí's best-known and best-loved poem – 'Mise Raifteirí an file …' ('I am Raftery the poet …'), also its title – will stir nostalgic memories in every Irish person of a certain age. For many years his poem was on the Irish primary school curriculum and learnt by heart by a generation. In the poem he describes his life as a blind poet and fiddle player travelling the west, entertaining people, but playing to 'empty pockets'.

Antoine Raifteirí was originally from Kiltimagh in Co. Mayo. At the age of 9 a bout of smallpox left him blind. He learnt to play the fiddle and, though illiterate, he had a way with words. He set off from Co. Mayo, intent on wandering the world, but only got as far as East Galway. In the bardic tradition of Celtic Ireland, he regaled the people of Gort and Loughrea with stories old and new, lyrical poems and songs. He plied his trade as a poet, wit and singer at weddings and gatherings, and in return was provided with shelter and food.

He died in a barn near Craughwell on Christmas Eve 1835, but his stories and poems did not die with him. The local people continued to recite his poems, which were saved for posterity when Lady Gregory began translating them with the help of a local farmer, Pat Mulkere, who had heard them from Raifteirí himself. Lady Gregory's interest in Raifteirí led her on a quest to find his resting place. In 1902 she found his grave at Killeenin Cemetery between Craughwell and Labane, and had it marked with a plaque.

Pádraic Ó'Conaire, Irish-Language Writer (1882–1928)

Pádraic Ó'Conaire was born in Galway city in 1882. Orphaned by the age of 11, he was sent to live with an uncle in Rosmuc. It was here that he learnt to speak Irish fluently. He was educated at Rockwell College and later Blackrock, where he was a classmate of Eamon de Valera, another staunch supporter of the Irish language.

In 1899 he left Ireland for London, where he worked as a civil servant. There he began writing in the Irish language, winning numerous prizes for his short stories. His best-known works are a short story entitled 'M'Asal Beag Dubh' ('My Little Black Donkey') and a novel, *Dreoráiocht* ('Exile'), the story of a Connemara man living in London.

Pádraic Ó'Conaire married Molly MacManus in London and they had four children. He decided to return to Ireland in 1915, to join the Irish Volunteers, leaving his family behind. Molly died in a German air raid on London in 1945.

Pádraic Ó'Conaire

In Ireland Ó'Conaire continued to write in Irish and had work published in the nationalist newspaper *An Claidheamh Soluis* ('Sword of Light'), which at the time was edited by Padraig Pearse.

From 1917 he took to the roads. Turning his back on his family, he embraced the tradition of the wandering bard. He wanted to mingle with the poor common people who inspired his work. Most of his stories from this period are sad and dark, reflecting his struggle with alcoholism. When he died, all he had with him was a pipe, tobacco and an apple. He is buried in Bohermore Cemetery.

Martín Ó'Direan, Irish-Language Poet (1910–1988)

Martín Ó'Direan was born on the Aran Islands and was a native Irish speaker. He joined the Irish civil service, working for the Post Office after leaving school, eventually moving to Dublin. He never lost his love of the Irish language and began writing poetry. He became established as a modern Irish-language poet after the publication of a collection of poems, *Rogha Dánta*. His poetry has been included in the Leaving Cert Irish curriculum.

An Irish-Language Television Station

The revival of the Irish language led to the national broadcasting company, RTÉ, setting up an Irish-language radio station, Radió na Gaeltachta, in 1972. Fittingly, the headquarters are not in Dublin, but are located in Casla, a Gaeltacht part of Connemara. By 2001 the station was operating twenty-four hours a day, nationwide. It was the second legal radio station to operate in Ireland after Radió Éireann.

By the mid-1990s, Ireland was ready for an Irish-language television station, which would also be operated by RTÉ. It was decided that, like the radio station, the broadcast studios should be outside Dublin and again the Connemara Gaeltacht was chosen. When it first began broadcasting on 31 October 1996 from studios at Baile na hAbhann, it was known as Teilfís na Gaeilge, abbreviated to T na G. In 1999 it was rebranded to its current name of TG4, as it was the fourth terrestrial television channel in Ireland.

THE PEOPLE AND PLACES OF THE CELTIC LITERARY REVIVAL

In the 1890s the coming together of a literary genius, an eccentric landowner and a widowed member of the landed gentry led to a movement which would change the direction of Irish literature.

In 1896 William Butler Yeats visited his friend Edward Martyn at Martyn's home, Tulira Castle, where he met Lady Augusta Gregory of Coole Park. Although they had met before, it was on this occasion that they recognised in each other kindred literary spirits. The Irish weather played its part in their founding of the Irish Literary Theatre. The three friends were visiting Doorus House near Kinvara, home of Martyn's cousin, Comte Florimonde de Basterot, one wet July afternoon in 1897. The typical west of Ireland rain kept them indoors by a blazing fire. Edward Martyn had written a play and was bemoaning the fact that there was no theatre company in Ireland producing plays written by Irish writers or based on Irish themes. They talked about setting up a theatre company of their own and from this conversation sprang the Irish Literary Theatre, later the Abbey Theatre. The Celtic Literary Revival was underway.

Many other writers joined the movement, all of whom visited Coole Park, many inspired by the culture and heritage of Co. Galway. On 8 May 1899 the Irish Literary Theatre opened its doors at the Antient Concert Rooms on what is now Pearse Street in Dublin. W.B. Yeats's *The Countess Cathleen* was the first play performed and on the second night Edward Martyn's *The Heather Field* was premiered. Both were well received, particularly the latter.

Lady Augusta Gregory and Coole Park

Isabella Augusta Persse was born at Roxborough House in 1852. The twelfth of sixteen children, her mother described her as the plainest of them all, and yet she would make the most advantageous marriage of any of her siblings. In 1880 she was married to Sir William Gregory of neighbouring Coole Park, former Member of Parliament for Galway, retired Governor of Ceylon and a man thirty-five years her senior.

The new Lady Gregory's brothers were delighted with the match as it allowed them to hunt the lands of Coole. For her it meant leaving behind a life of drudgery, tending to the breaks and scrapes of her brothers' fox hunting accidents, for a world of mixing with intellectuals in the drawing rooms of London. She was even presented to Queen Victoria.

In 1892 her husband died and once again her life changed. She wore widow's weeds for the rest of her days and dedicated herself to preserving Coole Park for her son Robert, born in 1881. Another Robert Gregory was the first of the family to come to Coole in the 1770s. He bought the estate with wealth amassed while working for the East India Company, built a Georgian mansion and planted what would become the Seven Woods of Coole, on the shores of the disappearing lake. The Potato Famine took its toll on the Gregorys and by the 1890s the estate was considerably reduced. To make ends meet, Lady Gregory turned to writing.

She began by editing her husband's autobiography, which was published in 1894. Encouraged by this, she turned to Irish folklore. She learnt Irish and made a number of visits to the Aran Islands. She was then able to translate the poems and stories recounted to her by the local Irish speakers of Coole.

Meeting William Butler Yeats was a significant event in her life. He encouraged her to write plays and to draw on the folklore of East Galway for inspiration. Together with Edward Martyn they founded the Irish Literary Theatre in 1899. In 1904 it became the Abbey Theatre and her play *Spreading the News* was performed on the opening night. She would write forty plays over her lifetime.

Her life was not without tragedy. Her favourite nephew, Sir Hugh Lane, was killed when the *Lusitania* was torpedoed by a German U-boat in 1915. The son of her sister Adelaide, he was a renowned art collector. Shortly before his death he had been appointed director of the National Gallery of Ireland. In his desk at the gallery, Lady Gregory found an unwitnessed codicil to his will stating that thirty-nine paintings in his collection should be left to Dublin, where a suitable gallery should be provided for their display. However, his official will left the paintings to the National Gallery in London. Lady Gregory became involved in a mission to secure the paintings for Dublin. Court cases ensued but she died in 1932, long before the affair was finally resolved in 1959. The settlement allowed for paintings to be kept at the Municipal Art Gallery in Dublin and the Tate in London and to be rotated every five years.

On 23 January 1918 Lady Gregory was once again bereaved. Her beloved son Robert was killed in Italy where he was serving with the Royal Flying Corps during the First World War. He is buried in Padua. Yeats wrote his poem 'An Irish Airman Foresees his Death' about Robert, who was survived by his wife Margaret and their three children, Richard, Katherine and Anne.

In 1927 Coole Park was sold to the Department of Lands and Agriculture, but Lady Gregory was allowed to live there for an annual rent of £100. Yeats remained a companion to Lady Gregory during her final years, when she was dying from cancer. He had briefly returned to Dublin when she passed away on 22 May 1932. She is buried at Bohermore Cemetery. After her death the house at Coole stood vacant until 1941, when it was demolished.

Edward Martyn and Tulira Castle

Edward Martyn's role in the Celtic Literary Revival is often overshadowed by his more famous co-founders. He was not as talented a writer as Yeats or Lady Gregory and in fact fell out with them over their criticism of one of his works. But his interests went beyond writing and included politics, the visual arts and music.

He was born at his mother's family home at Masonbrook, Loughrea in 1859. He was a neighbour of Lady Gregory, having inherited Tulira Castle while still a child. His mother sent him to Oxford University, and although he did not graduate, he came away with a deep appreciation of the importance of music, art and literature to society.

When Edward Martyn returned to Tulira from Oxford to take over the running of the estate, his mother decided it was time to refurbish the house. Tulira was transformed into a neo-Gothic mansion, incorporating the existing sixteenth-century tower keep. By the 1890s Edward Martyn was living there surrounded by the best of furnishings and modern art. Apart, that is, from his bedroom in the turret, which was decorated like a monastic cell.

William Butler Yeats was friendly with Edward Martyn and was invited to visit Tulira in 1896. Yeats warned his travelling companion, Arthur Symons, that as they were in the west of Ireland, he should not to be surprised if a barefoot servant greeted them at the door. But it was Yeats who was surprised by the Gothic mansion, the walls of which were adorned with Impressionist paintings and where the best of food and drink was served.

On another visit to Tulira a year later, Yeats met Lady Gregory, Edward Martyn's neighbour. They had encountered each other before but here they made a connection, which prompted her to invite Yeats to stay at her estate, Coole Park.

In 1897 Martyn wrote a play, *The Heather Field*, but there was no theatre in Ireland where it could be performed. He had his wish in 1899 when it was the second play ever performed by the fledgling Irish Literary Theatre. He was even more pleased that it was well received. Edward Martyn later fell out with his co-founders when they criticised another of his plays, and by the time the Abbey Theatre was opened in 1904 he was no longer involved.

A supporter of unionism in his student days, by the early 1900s Martyn was promoting the Irish nationalist cause. He wrote to the national newspapers in 1903 opposing the royal visit of King Edward VII. In 1905 when the nationalist political party Sinn Féin was founded by Arthur Griffith, Martyn became its first president.

A collector of art, Martyn was dismayed when he was unable to find high-quality Irish stained-glass windows for Labane church. He sourced windows in England and persuaded the artist Alfred Ernest Child to stay in Ireland and set up a school to train Irish artists in the craft. With the help of the portrait painter Sarah Purser, they set up An Túr Gloine stained glass studio in 1902, spreading the influence of the Celtic Revival to the visual arts.

Edward Martyn's real passion was music and particularly liturgical music. This led to him founding the Palestrina Boys' Choir at St Mary's Pro-Cathedral in Dublin. He also set up the Pipers Club, to revive and preserve traditional pipe music.

Regarded as an eccentric when he died in 1923, he left his body to science and asked that he be buried in a pauper's grave.

William Butler Yeats and Thoor Ballylee

William Butler Yeats is one of Ireland's best-known Anglo-Irish poets. Born in Dublin in 1865, he spent most of his childhood summers with his maternal grandparents in Co. Sligo. There he learnt the folklore and legends of Ireland, which would influence his early poetry.

Following his meeting with Lady Augusta Gregory, he was a regular visitor to Coole Park, near Gort. Their friendship was the driving force of the Celtic Literary Revival. He moved in literary circles and knew who should be invited to Coole to join the movement to further the progress of Irish literature. Although better-known as a poet, his first play, *The Land of Heart's Desire*, was performed in London in 1894. Yeats's play *The Countess Cathleen* opened the first season of the Irish Literary Theatre in 1899. By 1904 the movement had secured premises on Dublin's Abbey Street for a permanent theatre. On 27 December 1904 Yeats's play *On Baile's Strand* and Lady Gregory's *Spreading the News* were performed there.

He was a staunch defender of the theatre and the work of his fellow playwrights. The premier of John Millington Synge's *Playboy of the Western World* caused riots in the audience in 1907 and when Sean O'Casey's 1928 play *The Plough and the Stars* caused further riots, Yeats took to the stage to berate the audience, famously telling them that they had 'disgraced themselves again'.

The peaceful surroundings of Coole Park provided Yeats with inspiration. He would wander the woods humming to himself as he developed the rhythm for a new poem. Perhaps he hummed 'The Wild Swans at Coole' as he made his way back to the house after a visit to Coole's turlough.

In 1917, the year in which he married George Hyde-Lees, Yeats was looking for a home in Co. Galway and bought Thoor Ballylee for £35. The once-ruined de Burgo tower was built on the banks of the Streamstown River on the Coole Park estate. The tower had been refurbished in the 1800s, with a thatched cottage added to it, but had been vacant for a number of years. Yeats engaged William A. Scott, then Professor of Architecture at the National University of Ireland, to refurbish both tower and cottage. He referred to Scott as 'that drunken man of genius'.

Yeats saw Thoor Ballylee as a place of his own, a country retreat for his wife and later his two children. But he did not spend as much time as he had hoped there. The turbulent political environment of Ireland in the early 1920s, his growing commitments and health problems kept him away from Galway.

Thoor Ballylee did, however, serve as a source of inspiration for Yeats, and in 1928 he published a volume of poetry entitled *The Tower*, followed in 1933 by a volume entitled *The Winding Stairs*.

In addition to spending time at Coole, Yeats also visited Connemara. He spent his honeymoon at Renvyle House, the home of his friend Oliver St John Gogarty. The pair had literature and writing in common, but the eminent surgeon had also extracted the poet's tonsils.

After Yeats' death in 1939, as he predicted in the words he had carved on a plaque on the tower wall, Thoor Ballylee fell once again into disrepair. It was restored as a museum in 1965. Its proximity to the fast-flowing Streamstown river has meant that Thoor Ballylee is prone to considerable winter flooding. Today it is maintained by Fáilte Ireland.

The Autograph Tree at Coole Park

After her marriage to Sir William Gregory, Lady Gregory found herself gracing the elegant drawing rooms of London. Rubbing shoulders with the great and good of British society, she could not help being star struck. She began collecting autographs of those she met on her fans. One fan bears the signatures of James MacNeill Whistler (painter), Sir Randolph Churchill (father of Winston) and William Gladstone (British Prime Minister), while another has the signatures of famous writers including Henry James, Mark Twain, Thomas Hardy and Rudyard Kipling.

As she began hosting the cream of Irish literary talent at Coole Park, Lady Gregory encouraged her guests to carve their initials into the bark of a copper beech tree in the walled garden, for posterity. She was very particular about who she allowed to engrave the Autograph Tree, although some locals did manage to get their names on there. Once she chased away a group of American students trying to carve their names onto it, and then regretted it as she could have chased away a future president or successful writer.

The Autograph Tree is a who's who of the Celtic Literary Revival.

Violet Martin, Writer (1861–1915)

W.B. Yeats carved Violet Martin's initials onto the Autograph Tree as she looked on, smoking a cigarette. Violet Martin was brought up at Ross Castle near Oughterard. Descended from the Martin Tribe of Galway, she co-wrote a series of books with her Cork cousin Edith Somerville under the pen name 'Martin Ross'.

The two cousins did not meet each other until they were in their twenties, when Violet's mother brought her to visit the Somervilles at Drishane House in Castletownshend. They shared an interest in horses and writing. Combining their talents, their first book, *The Real Cousin*, was published in 1889. Their best-known works are 'The Irish R.M.' (Resident Magistrate) series and *The Real Charlotte*. The Irish R.M. books humorously recount the interactions between the fox-hunting-mad landed gentry, the local Irish and an English gentleman sent to keep law and order.

Edith came up with the stories, but it was Violet's wit and humour which made the books such a success. Initially their families frowned on their commercial activity, but soon changed their minds when the venture provided money for both cash-strapped families.

Violet had a hunting accident in 1898, which left her semi-invalided. By 1906 she was living alone at Ross Castle and decided to move permanently to Castletownshend to live with Edith. She died there in 1915, from a brain tumour. They had written sixteen books together. Edith continued to write and published her work under the name 'Somerville and Ross', believing that Violet's spirit was still with her.

John Millington Synge, Writer (1871–1909)
Another prominent figure to initial the Autograph Tree was John Millington Synge. An aspiring writer from Dublin, he thought he would pursue a career in music, but decided he was better suited to writing. On a visit to Paris in December 1896 he met and became friendly with W.B. Yeats. Struggling to find a genre, Yeats advised him to go the Aran Islands. There, isolated from urban distractions, maybe he would find inspiration.

He first went to the Aran Islands in 1898 and would spend the next five summers there, particularly on Inishmaan. He was intrigued by the way of life and the stories of the islanders but also by the Hiberno English, the particular dialect of English spoken by native Irish speakers.

He was soon writing plays and visiting Coole Park. His first two plays, *Riders to the Sea* and *The Well of Saints*, were not well received.

In 1904 when the Abbey Theatre was founded he became a co-director with Lady Gregory and Yeats. Because Synge was the only director actually living in Dublin, he became involved in the day-to-day running of the theatre.

His best-known play is *The Playboy of the Western World*, which was first performed at the Abbey Theatre in 1907. The play caused riots, as many nationalists saw it as offensive and an insult to Ireland. They were not happy with the negative portrayal of the people of the west, and found the subject of patricide particularly hard to take. When the Abbey toured America in 1911, the cast of *Playboy* were arrested in Philadelphia as the play was deemed obscene and immoral. They were all later released without charge.

Synge died at the age of 37 from Hodgkin's Disease. He was working on a new play, *Deirdre of the Sorrows*, which Yeats later completed.

George Moore, Writer (1852–1933)
Another name engraved on the Autograph Tree is that of George Moore from Moore Hall in Co. Mayo. A cousin of Edward Martyn, he was a novelist, playwright and poet. His best-known work is *Confessions of a Young Man*. He also collaborated with Yeats, most notably on the play *Diarmuid and Grania* in 1901.

George Bernard Shaw, Playwright (1856–1950)
Shaw and his wife were regular visitors to Coole Park. He was a particular favourite of Lady Gregory's grandchildren because he would play with them, although they did accuse him of cheating during a game of 'hunt the thimble'. At breakfast one morning, the children were horrified to see him spreading jam on one side of his toast and butter on the other. Due to rationing during the First World War, Lady Gregory had insisted that visitors could have one or the other at breakfast. Shaw claimed that he was not breaking the rules.

Sean O'Casey, Playwright (1880–1964)
Lady Gregory's grandchildren were most impressed with Sean O'Casey's carving on the Autograph Tree. He told them that he had plenty of practice, having carved his initials on the doors of tenement houses in his youth.

Unlike other writers of the Celtic Literary Revival, O'Casey came from a poor background, having grown up in the tenement slums of Dublin. He was the first of the group to write about contemporary issues, such as the 1916 Easter Rising in *The Plough and the Stars*.

Other names on the tree include: Dr Douglas Hyde (1860–1949); artist Jack Butler Yeats (1871–1957); publisher, poet and artist George William Russell, who wrote under the pseudonym AE (1867–1935); and artist Augustus John (1878–1961).

THEATRES OF GALWAY

Early Theatres

The earliest known theatre in Galway was on Kirwan's Lane in the city. In 1783 Richard 'Humanity Dick' Martin, who had a townhouse nearby, funded the theatre for his wife, Elizabeth Vasey. It could accommodate 100 people, as long as ladies did not wear hoops. Theobald Wolfe Tone, a tutor of Martin's half-brothers, appeared in two plays. He was an admirer of Mrs Martin. The theatre continued to host performances until at least the 1820s.

By the end of the nineteenth century the Racquet Court Theatre on Middle Street was the main theatre in Galway city. Count John McCormack performed there.

The Taibhdhearc Theatre

The word 'Taibhdhearc' translates as 'ghostly vision' and is the name of the national Irish-language theatre based in Galway. Founded in 1928 (towards the end of the Celtic Literary Revival), the theatre company leased the Augustinian Hall on Middle Street. After fire damage in the 1980s, the theatre was refurbished as a modern 148-seat venue on the original site.

The first play to be performed was Micheal MacLiammoir's *Diarmud agus Gráinne*. Not only did he write the play, he designed the set and costumes. He also painted two peacocks on the stage curtains, which are still there to this day.

The Druid Theatre

Galway's most famous professional theatre company is The Druid, the first such group to be based outside of Dublin. Two of its founders, Marie Mullen and Garry Hynes, graduated from UCG in 1975 and they set up The Druid with Mick Lally, a teacher and actor at the Taibhdhearc.

In 1979 they found a permanent home on Courthouse Lane, now Druid Lane. The company has toured all over Ireland and around the world. Its most ambitious undertaking was a performance of all six of J.M. Synge's plays in one day, during the Galway Arts Festival in 2005.

Macnas

Macnas ('joyful abandonment') is a performance group founded in Galway in 1986. Macnas has broken the boundaries of street theatre with giant puppets, the most iconic of which are the oversized heads of the four members of U2, which toured with the band on their Zooropa Tour in 1993. Every Halloween weekend, Macnas parades a show involving hundreds of volunteers and impressive puppetry through the streets of Galway.

GALWAY AND THE FILM INDUSTRY

The unspoilt scenery of Connemara, the dramatic cliffs of the Aran Islands, the coastline of hidden beaches, the quiet harbours and the quaint country towns have attracted film-makers to Galway since the 1930s.

In 1989 the first Galway Film Fleadh was held in conjunction with the Galway Arts Festival. It has since become an internationally recognised film event. Many Irish films have premiered at the Film Fleadh, most notably *Once* in 2006, which went on to win an Oscar for Best Original Song in 2008.

When the Irish Film Board was set up in 1993, it was fitting that it should have its headquarters in Galway. It is a state-run body tasked with funding and supporting Irish film-makers, and also promotes Ireland as a location for foreign producers and directors.

The National University of Ireland Galway (NUIG) opened the Huston School of Film and Digital Media in 2003. The film director John Huston had a long association with Co. Galway. In 1951 he bought St Clerans House near Craughwell, refurbished it and moved his family, including his famous actor daughter Anjelica, to live there. He became an Irish citizen in 1964, such was his love of Ireland and particularly Co. Galway.

In 2010 the Huston family donated John Huston's archive, which consists of screenplay drafts, scripts and other film-related material, to the NUIG. The archive is held in the Hardiman Library.

In 2014, Galway city was designated a UNESCO World Heritage City of Film, one of eight worldwide, in recognition of the long history of film-making in the region. Galway is only the second Irish city to receive a UNESCO World Heritage designation – Dublin is a UNESCO World Heritage City of Literature.

FILMS FEATURING GALWAY

Man of Aran (1934)

The earliest film associated with Galway is Robert Flaherty's *Man of Aran* (1934). He travelled to the Aran Islands intent on making a film that depicted the harsh realities of life on an island on the western seaboard of Europe. He used the locals as actors, and he is said to have paid them with a keg of porter and £5 each. One of the pivotal scenes follows the locals as they hunt a basking shark. Not only were the scenes incredibly dangerous to film, they were not exactly authentic. In the past, islanders had hunted basking sharks for the oil they could retrieve from the creature's liver. But this tradition had died out during the middle of the 1800s as the islanders adopted paraffin oil for lighting purposes. A fisherman from Galway's Claddagh had to be brought out to the islands to show them what to do.

The Quiet Man (1952)

The best-known film made in Galway is John Ford's *The Quiet Man*, starring Maureen O'Hara and John Wayne. The village of Cong, parts of which are in Co. Mayo, thrived on its association with the film for years afterwards. The railway station at Ballyglunin between Tuam and Athenry also featured in the film. Ford was coming back to his roots. Born John Martin Feeney in Maine in 1894, his father was from Spiddal, a descendant of the Morris tribe and his mother was from Kilronan on Inishmore.

Alfred the Great (1968)

In 1968 most of *Alfred the Great* was filmed in Co. Galway. It stars David Hemmings as the Wessex Saxon king. Other cast members include Michael York, Ian McKellen, Christopher Timothy and Sinead Cusack. The film was not a success.

Flight of the Doves (1971)

Flight of the Doves is based on a novel by Galway writer Walter Maken. The film features Athenry Castle and starred Ron Moody paired with child star Jack Wild. They had previously worked together on the film *Oliver*.

The Mackintosh Man (1973)

The village of Roundstone features in John Huston's *The Mackintosh Man* starring Paul Newman and James Mason. Scenes were filmed at Roundstone Pier and on Galway Bay.

North Sea Hijack (1980)

James Mason appears in another film that features Co. Galway. In *North Sea Hijack*, Dunguaire Castle in Kinvara features as a Scottish castle. Roger Moore and Anthony Perkins also star.

The Field (1990)

Jim Sheridan's *The Field* was filmed in the area of Leenane. One of the main scenes occurs at Aaslagh Falls. The film was based on the play of the same name written by Kerry playwright John B. Keane. Four of the film's actors were nominated for Oscars: Richard Harris, John Hurt, Tom Berenger and Brenda Fricker. Brenda Fricker was the only one to win the iconic statuette.

Into the West (1991)

Into the West is the story of two young boys from Dublin whose horse is stolen and follows their adventure as they head west to retrieve him. The film stars Gabriel Byrne, Ellen Barkin and Connemara.

The Matchmaker (1997)

The Matchmaker is the story of an American sent to Ireland in search of her politician boss's Irish ancestry. She arrives in an Irish village as a Matchmaking Festival is taking place. Roundstone and Inishmore were used as locations. Janeane Garofalo and Milo O'Shea star.

Leap Year (2010)
Connemara and the Aran Islands feature in the 'chick flick' *Leap Year*. The film stars Amy Adams and Matthew Goode.

The Guard (2011)
The Guard is a more recent film set entirely in Galway. Starring Brendan Gleeson as the eponymous policeman, this dark comedy thriller features Salthill, Barna and Connemara.

TELEVISION SHOWS SET IN GALWAY

Single Handed
Police drama *Single Handed* ran for thirteen episodes between 2007 and 2010 and was filmed in many locations around Connemara, including Tully Cross, the location for the police station.

Jack Taylor
Jack Taylor is a series following the exploits of a private investigator played by English actor Ian Glenn. The series is set and filmed in Galway city and is very popular in Germany.

Ros na Rún
Ros na Rún is an Irish-language soap opera set in a fictitious village in Co. Galway. It was first aired in 1996 and is still running on TG4. It is filmed mainly in and around Spiddal.

THE SONGS OF GALWAY

Galway has a rich tradition of music with many songs extolling the beauty of the county and, most recently, the beauty of its girls!

'Galway Bay'
'Galway Bay' is the most famous song about Galway. It was made famous when the Hollywood star Bing Crosby recorded it. However, its composer never made a penny from the song.

It was written by Dr Arthur Colahan, who grew up in Galway but by the 1920s was living in England. In 1927 he composed 'Galway Bay', which was just one of many songs he composed about Ireland. He did not write his compositions down, consigning them instead to memory and singing them regularly. He was heard singing 'Galway Bay' by a music promoter, who wrote it down and somehow it was sent to Bing Crosby. It featured in *The Quiet Man* and has since been recorded by many other artists, including a parody version by the Clancy Brothers.

Some of Dr Colahan's original lyrics were changed. He referred to the 'English' coming to Ireland and trying to teach the Irish their ways. Today the song refers to them as 'Strangers'.

'The Fields of Athenry'

The M6 motorway near Athenry is surrounded by small, low-lying fields, lined with stone walls. This gentle rural landscape inspired Pete St John to write the classic ballad 'The Fields of Athenry' in the 1970s. There have been many recordings of the song, but the most successful was folk singer Paddy Reilly's version, which was recorded in 1982. It did not reach the number one slot in the Irish music chart, but it stayed in the charts for seventy weeks.

The song is a plaintive Famine ballad. Michael has been caught stealing 'Trevelyn's Corn' and the penalty is transportation to Australia. Left behind, his wife and young family now find it 'lonely around the Fields of Athenry'.

The anthem-like chorus has made the song popular with supporters of various sports teams. It is regularly sung from the terraces of stadia around Ireland and the world in support of Irish teams. To date, the supporters of the Republic of Ireland international soccer team, the Irish international rugby team, Munster's rugby team and Connacht's rugby team can all be heard belting out 'The Fields of Athenry'. Most counties in Ireland will lay claim to the song as nowhere in Ireland escaped the effects of the Potato Famine of the 1840s, but it is particularly dear to the hearts of Galwegians.

'N17'

In 1991 a little-known Tuam band called the Saw Doctors released their first album *If this is Rock and Roll, I Want My Old Job Back*. On that album were two of what would become the band's best-known and best-loved songs. 'I Us'ta Love Her' spent nine weeks at number one in the Irish charts that year. 'N17' reminisces about travelling on the eponymous road, the main road between Tuam and Galway. The green fields are lined by grey stone walls referenced in the song and the traveller feels a lump in his throat as he turns left at Claregalway to take the road leading to Shannon from where he is emigrating to London or America. The song was an anthem for a generation of Irish emigrants.

'Galway Girl'

The song was written by the American songwriter Steve Earle in 2008 and became a big hit for Mundy and Sharon Shannon. The song refers to the Long Walk and the Salthill Prom in Galway city. It featured in the film *P.S. I Love You*.

And still the songs about Galway keep coming. In 2017 Ed Sheeran included a song called 'Galway Girl' on his 2017 album, *Divide*. The video, featuring the actress Saoirse Ronan, was filmed in Galway and saw Sheeran return to the streets where he had once been a busker.

7

BATTLES, WAR
AND DISASTERS

Much of Ireland's turbulent history has been punctuated with wars, battles and risings. Some of Ireland's bloodiest battles were fought in Co. Galway and many brave soldiers hailed from the county. Galway has also experienced its fair share of disasters.

THE BATTLE OF ATHENRY (1316)

In 1315 the brothers Rory and Felim O'Connor were at war with each other. They were each vying for the kingship of Connacht. Rory defeated his brother and became King of Connacht. He immediately aligned himself with Edward Bruce, who had come to Ireland with the backing of his brother, King Robert I of Scotland, intent on establishing himself as King of Ireland and overthrowing the Anglo-Normans.

By the early fourteenth century the Anglo-Normans had established themselves in the south-east of Connacht with settlements at Galway, Athenry and Loughrea. Conscious of the hostility of the Gaelic chieftains, these towns were surrounded by protective walls – and in the case of Loughrea, a moat, which still exists today. On 10 August 1316 Felim O'Connor led his clan and five other Gaelic families – the O'Shaughnessys, the O'Heynes, the O'Kellys, the O'Flahertys and the O'Rourkes – in an attack on Athenry. Sir Richard de Bermingham, 4th Baron of Athenry and William Laith de Burgo, the Red Earl's cousin, were ready for them. With their superior arms, the

Anglo-Norman barons won the battle. It is thought that 7,000 died at the Battle of Athenry. Felim O'Connor was killed along with five other Gaelic chieftains. The Battle of Athenry brought an end to the power of the O'Connors in the west. The walls of Athenry were rebuilt after the battle and paid for by selling the armour of the defeated Gaelic lords.

THE BATTLE OF KNOCKDOE (1504)

This little-known battle saw Irish chieftains pitched against each other in a power struggle for control of Ireland.

In the west Ulick Burke, Chief of Clanricarde, was keen to establish his authority in Connacht. He was a descendant of the de Burgos who had founded the city of Galway and had 'gone native' and becoming more Irish than the Irish themselves by the sixteenth century. In the east of Ireland, Gerald Fitzgerald, Earl of Kildare was appointed Lord Deputy of Ireland by King Henry VII, and as such was the lord of Gaelic Ireland. In an attempt to curtail the unruly Burke's power, the Lord Deputy sent his daughter Eustacia to Connacht to marry him.

This made no difference to Burke. In fact, he sent her back, as he preferred his adulterous relationship with the wife of O'Kelly, Lord of Hymany. To further upset O'Kelly, Burke raided three of his castles: Castleblakney, Garbally and Monivea. With the aid of his allies, the O'Briens of Thomond, the MacNamaras, the O'Kennedys and the O'Carrolls of Ely, Burke then went on to sack Galway and Athenry. It was these actions that led to a battle being fought on a fine August day on the slope of a hill near Lackagh, Knockdoe ('the Hill of the Axes').

The Lord Deputy marched west with an army of 6,000. He was supported by the O'Kelly's, much aggrieved by Burke's antics, and other Gaelic clans from Connacht, including the MacWilliam Burkes, kinsmen of Ulick Burke and the O'Neills, and the O'Donnells from Ulster.

All of Ireland was involved in this conflict. There was no clear division of Anglo-Norman versus Gaelic Irish. Clans of Connacht were engaged on both sides, and both sides enlisted the services of Scottish mercenaries, known as 'Gallowglasses', equipped with swords and axes.

Ulick Burke and his supporters literally had an uphill battle that day. To add to their woes, they were facing into the blinding sun. The battle went on all day, but in the end the Earl of Kildare came out victorious. It is said that 4,000 men died at the Battle of Knockdoe. Ulick Burke had his castle and lands at Claregalway confiscated and his children were kidnapped in the hope of encouraging him to refrain from causing any more trouble.

While the weapon of choice of the Gallowglasses who fought on both sides of the Battle of Knockdoe was the axe, someone on the battlefield that day discharged a firearm. It is the first record of a firearm being used in the west of Ireland.

The Battle of Knockdoe brought an end to the powers of Gaelic families in the west of Ireland. In recognition of the part played by the Fitzgeralds of Kildare in the victory, their coat of arms was carved into the walls of the newly built Lynch's Castle in Galway city.

THE BATTLE OF AUGHRIM (1691)

In 1688, the Catholic King James II fled London, allegedly throwing the Great Seal, the symbol of his monarchy, into the Thames as he fled. The Glorious Revolution was underway and James's daughter Mary ascended the throne with her Dutch husband William of Orange. In Mary II and William III, the English Parliament finally had the Protestant monarchy it wanted.

King James II fled to Catholic France but was determined to retrieve his throne. He returned to the British Isles in 1689, coming in by way of Bantry Bay, Co. Cork. As Ireland still had a large Catholic population, he knew he could drum up support for a campaign against his son-in-law. Things went well until he reached the city of Derry, where the gates were slammed shut in his face. William eventually arrived in Ireland and the two kings came face to face in battle across the River Boyne on 12 July 1690.

There the Jacobites, James's supporters (from the Latin for James, *Jacomus*), were defeated by the Williamites. James II returned to France and William III to London, but the war raged on in Ireland.

A siege at Athlone, along the Shannon, resulted in another Jacobite loss. Once again in retreat, Charles Chalmont, Marquis of St Ruth, the French general leading the Jacobite forces, decided to make a stand against the Williamites at the village of Aughrim, outside Ballinasloe, on 12 July 1691. Patrick Sarsfield, leader of the Irish forces, advised against this, but St Ruth would not be swayed.

At the outset of the battle General St Ruth appeared to have the advantage. He positioned his 20,000 soldiers on a hill in front of a bog. The Williamites, led by the Dutch general Godert Ginkel, made use of a narrow causeway through the bog on St Ruth's left flank. It is said that the exploding cannon balls could be heard as far away as Galway.

Local lore has it that Williamite soldier John Trench directed a cannon at General St Ruth, decapitating him. The loss of their leader sent the Jacobites into disarray, and they eventually lost the battle. It is said that 7,000 Jacobite supporters and 1,000 Williamites died at what was to be the bloodiest battle ever fought in Ireland. Many of the dead were left to rot unburied on the battlefield. St Ruth's headless body was brought to Loughrea, where his interment in a tomb at the Carmelite Abbey in the dead of night was witnessed by five priests.

Patrick Sarsfield managed to escape after the Battle of Aughrim. He retreated to Limerick, where the Jacobites took an unsuccessful last stand against the Williamites. The siege culminated in the Treaty of Limerick, which brought an end to the struggle to replace the Jacobite king on the throne. Many of those who had supported King James were penalised, their lands confiscated. Peter Martin of the Woodlawn estate near Aughrim had supported the Catholic cause and lost his estates to John Trench, the man who allegedly killed General St Ruth.

A MURDEROUS YEAR IN GALWAY (1882)

The year 1882 was a turbulent one in Ireland, and particularly in Galway. The Land War was creating friction between tenants and landlords and the Land League's encouragement of tenants to refuse to pay unfair rents was causing much agitation.

Lough Mask Murders

On 3 January 1882 Joseph Huddy was going about his business. In his capacity as a bailiff on Lord Ardilaun's estate, he was going to Cloughbrack, near Lough Mask, to serve eviction notices on some houses there. Accompanying him was his 16-year-old grandson, John Huddy. They disappeared in broad daylight. Twenty-three days later their bodies were found in the lake. Both men had been shot. Three locals, one of whom was to be served an eviction notice on the day the Huddys disappeared, were tried and found guilty of the Lough Mask murders.

The Lord Lieutenant

In another murderous incident that year, John Henry Blake, the agent for Lord Clanricarde's estates, was murdered on his way to church in Loughrea.

When the Lord Lieutenant for Ireland, Lord Cavendish, was murdered along with his deputy in Dublin's Phoenix Park in the May of 1882, people thought they had seen the worst of what appeared to be a lawless Ireland.

There was worse to come and again in Galway.

The Maamtrasna Murders

On the night of 17 August 1882, a group of men stormed into the cottage of John Joyce, a sheep farmer in the region of Maamtrasna in north Co. Galway. They shot John and two of his sons and bludgeoned his wife, mother and daughter to death. One son, Patsy, survived the attack but was unable to identify the culprits.

Three days after the murders, three cousins of the Joyce family came forward and said they had seen ten men approach the cottage that night, and were able to name some of them. They alleged that three of the group entered the cottage and murdered the family.

In the wake of the escalating violence in the county, the authorities were anxious to settle the case. Ten men were rounded up, put in a steamboat and sent to the prison in Galway. While the police were pleased to have suspects, that is all they had, as the three witnesses could not identify which of the ten had actually entered the cottage.

Two of the suspects were pressured to turn Queen's evidence. Anthony Philbin and Thomas Casey changed their testimony. In Philbin's case, it later came to light that he had been at a wake that night and had not been at Maamtrasna. In Casey's revised testimony, he said that seven men had been there on the night of the murders and identified Pat Casey, Pat Joyce and Myles Joyce as the murderers. He also said that some of the men involved were still at large. This suggested that some of those now in prison were innocent.

The trial was held in Dublin in November 1882. Most of the eight accused were native Irish speakers, but the trial was held in English, with a policeman drafted in to act as an interpreter. The defence lawyer was inexperienced and made no attempt to challenge contradictions in witnesses' evidence or to establish a motive for the murders.

Pat Joyce, Pat Casey and Myles Joyce were all found guilty and sentenced to execution by hanging. The remaining suspects were encouraged to plead guilty and thereby avoid the fate of their co-accused. All pleaded guilty and all were sentenced to twenty years in prison.

By now the case was headline news in Ireland and Britain. Everyone had an opinion, including Queen Victoria, who thought that all ten should be hanged.

All were returned to Galway Prison, where a gallows was prepared for 15 December. A couple of days before he was to die, Pat Joyce signed a written testimony admitting to killing the Joyces of Maamtrasna. He stated that Myles Joyce was not involved and had not been present that night. Myles had continued to proclaim his innocence and his wife said he had been with her all night.

Word was sent to Dublin about this new evidence but John Poyntz Spencer, 5th Earl Spencer, Lord Lieutenant of Ireland 1882–1885, the Queen's representative and a good friend of Gladstone, refused to change the death penalty.

On 15 December Myles Joyce was hanged alongside Pat Joyce and Pat Casey.

Thomas Casey, whose revised testimony had led to the convictions, returned to Maamtrasna but was treated like an outcast. He approached the local priest and he proclaimed in front of a church congregation and the Bishop of Tuam, Dr MacEvilly, that he had been at Maamtrasna on the night of the murders and Myles Joyce had not.

The inquiry demanded by the bishop was refused but then politicians took up the case. In October 1884 the matter was debated in the House of Commons. Sir Randolph Churchill, Gladstone and Parnell all had their say on the matter. The motion to open an inquiry into the mishandling and the miscarriage of justice in the Maamtrasna Murders was defeated.

Why were the Joyce family murdered? No one knows. Perhaps John Joyce had been stealing sheep, maybe he had threatened to go to the police with evidence of a secret organisation or maybe someone in the family knew something about the earlier murders of the Huddys. But the story continues – following a review of Myles Joyce's conviction by an eminent academic, in April 2018 President Michael D. Higgins granted Myles Joyce a Presidential Pardon.

Galway and the Easter Rising of 1916

The long-awaited Home Rule Bill was passed through the British Houses of Parliament in 1912. Its implementation would provide Ireland with a devolved parliament in Dublin for oversight of Ireland's internal affairs. But not everyone in Ireland was happy about this turn of events.

The Protestant community, particularly those in the north-east, saw Home Rule as 'Rome Rule' and pledged to use force to prevent it being implemented. The Ulster Volunteer Army was formed, filling its ranks from the ordinary people of Ulster, who set about arming themselves for possible conflict.

In the south, where there was majority support for the Home Rule Bill, the Irish Volunteer Army was founded in 1913 as a direct response to the establishment of the Ulster Volunteer Army. Behind the scenes, the Irish Republican Brotherhood (IRB), a secret Fenian organisation, was taking advantage of this call to arms and by 1915 was preparing the Irish Volunteers for a rebellion. Thousands of Galway men joined the Irish Volunteers. They were mainly young farmers who were members of the Gaelic Athletic Association or the Gaelic League. While their motivation was mainly patriotic, Galway was still a poor farming county, where the distribution of land was causing agitation.

In East Galway, Tom Kenny, a blacksmith from Craughwell, was the main IRB man. He did not take kindly to the IRB Committee sending a 22-year-old member from Dublin to train the Irish Volunteers for rebellion in 1914. But Liam Mellows eventually gained the respect of the locals. He made his headquarters in Athenry, where he set up a rifle range in the local town hall for target practice.

As the date for the Rising approached, the plans went awry. The *Aud*, a ship carrying a consignment of rifles destined for the rebels, was intercepted by the British Navy off the coast of Co. Kerry on Good Friday 1916.

Without the weapons, the leader of the Irish Volunteer Army, Eoin MacNeill, countermanded the plan for the Easter Rising. From this point on, confusion reigned. The leaders of the IRB, based in Dublin, sent out word that the Rising would take place on Easter Monday, 24 April.

On that day, almost 1,000 members of the Irish Volunteers rose out in east Co. Galway, the biggest number of Volunteers to mobilise outside of Dublin. Led by Liam Mellows, some attacked the RIC barracks at Clarinbridge, while another group attacked the RIC station at Oranmore. In an effort to disrupt communication with Galway, the rebels dug up part of the railway line between Galway and Athenry. These attacks were unsuccessful, as reinforcements of the RIC and the Connaught Rangers Regiment arrived from Galway.

By late Tuesday evening, between 500 and 700 Volunteers, mainly from Craughwell, Clarinbridge, Oranmore and Athenry had gathered at Athenry's agricultural college to await orders. On Wednesday, a group of Volunteers from Claregalway and Castlegar were attacked by the RIC near Carnmore, during which skirmish RIC Constable Patrick Whelan was killed. His last words had been a plea to the Volunteers to give themselves up: 'Surrender boys, I know ye all.' He was the only fatality in Galway during Easter week. These Volunteers fled Carnmore and joined Liam Mellows in Athenry.

Galway city had not come out in sympathy with the rebels. Nevertheless, martial law had been declared and the city readied itself for an attack from the Irish Volunteers. The British Army secured strategic buildings such as the Post Office. By mid-week, the Royal Navy had four warships in Galway Bay. HMS *Guillemot*, HMS *Laburnum*, HMS *Gloucester* and HMS *Snowdrop* began bombarding the areas to the east of the city, where most of the rebel activity had occurred.

Midweek, Mellows and Kenny retreated to Moyode Castle near Craughwell with about 300 Volunteers, others having gone home. There was only a caretaker on the premises, and the castle was easily taken. Tom Kenny wanted to continue the fight by stealing livestock and securing land, but when word arrived on Saturday 29 April that the Dublin Volunteers had surrendered, the Galway Volunteers dispersed.

This was not the end. Many of those involved in the Galway Rising were rounded up and sent to prisons in Britain; 322 of the 1,800 prisoners held in Frongoch in North Wales were from Galway. By Christmas 1916 most had been released and were back home.

Liam Mellows fled to Co. Clare and was in hiding until he sailed from Queenstown in Cork in October, to Liverpool and then to New York. He returned to Ireland when independence was eventually granted. He supported Eamon de Valera in his opposition to the Anglo-Irish Treaty of 1921 and was executed during the Civil War for his anti-Treaty stance.

GALWAY MILITARY

Many Galway men served with the British Army, a large number joining the Connaught Rangers. Three Irish men have been awarded the Victoria Cross for their bravery.

Cornelius Coughlan, Victoria Cross Recipient (1828–1915)
Cornelius Coughlan was born in Eyrecourt, where he completed his education and then decided to join the British Army. In 1857, he was wounded in India while attempting the brave rescue of a fellow injured soldier during the Indian Mutiny. He was awarded his VC in 1863. He returned to Ireland and lived out his days in Westport, and was a reservist in the Connaught Rangers.

When he died in 1915, Westport gave him a military funeral. However, a year later, the Easter Rising and subsequent events meant that those who had served in the British Army were forgotten and ignored. It was not until 2004 that a headstone was placed on Cornelius Coughlan's grave.

Thomas Grady, Victoria Cross Recipient (1835–1901)
Thomas Grady was from the Claddagh in Galway. He was recommended twice for a Victoria Cross for acts of bravery under fire at Sebastopol during the Crimean War, in 1854. He was eventually awarded the VC in 1857. He died in Melbourne, Australia.

Alexander Young, Victoria Cross Recipient (1873–1916)
Alexander Young was born in Clarinbridge but grew up in Oranmore. He joined the British Army and was sent to India, where he worked as a riding instructor. He was nominated for a VC for his bravery whilst serving in South Africa during the Boer War in 1901, where he captured a Boer commandant.

Alexander was killed at the Battle of the Somme in 1916 and has no known grave.

First World War
Of the 40,000 Irishmen who were killed whilst serving for the British Army during the First World War, 755 came from Galway city and county.

The Connaught Rangers

The 88th Royal Regiment of the Connaught Rangers was founded by John Thomas de Burgh, 13th Earl of Clanricarde in 1793, in response to the threat posed by Napoleon. It was feared that he might try to invade Britain via Ireland. The regiment recruited men mainly from the western provinces, although men from other parts of the country also joined.

Over a period of almost 130 years, the Connaught Rangers fought in Europe, Asia and South Africa. During the First World War members fought in France, Flanders, Mesopotamia and at Gallipoli.

On 28 June 1920 soldiers of the Connaught Rangers serving at Jullundur in the Punjab, India, laid down their weapons and refused to carry out their duties because of the atrocities being carried out in Ireland by the Black and Tans. Their mutiny spread to Solon, where other soldiers of the regiment were stationed. They handed over their weapons. In a bid to retrieve them from the armoury, two soldiers, Private Patrick Smythe from Drogheda, Co. Louth and Private Peter Sears from Ballinrobe, Co. Mayo, were killed. This brought an end to the mutiny, the last in the British army. Of the 500 or so soldiers who mutinied, sixty-two were court-martialled. One, Private James Daly from Tyrellspass, Co. Westmeath, was executed. He claimed that he had led the mutiny.

In 1922 the regiment was disbanded under the terms of the Anglo-Irish Treaty of 1921. The regimental colours were presented to King George V at Windsor Castle. Older colours hang in St Nicholas' Collegiate Church, Galway.

Fifty years after the mutiny, the remains of the three dead soldiers were repatriated to Ireland. James Daly was buried in Tyrellspass, while the other two were buried in Glasnevin Cemetery in Dublin.

DISASTERS

Titanic *and the Galway Connection*

J. Bruce Ismay (1862–1937) was chairman and managing director of the White Star Shipping Line in the early 1900s. His ambition was to build a ship that would win the Blue Ribband, the prize for the fastest Atlantic crossing. The Cunard Line, his main rival, had won the prize with the *Lusitania*. White Star decided to build a new ship which would not only be the fastest ever built, but she would also be unsinkable.

Titanic was built in the Harland and Wolff Dockyards in Belfast and was launched in 1911. Ismay was heavily involved in the planning, design and construction of the liner. He made the devastating decision to reduce the number of lifeboats on board from 46 to 16. His argument was that extra lifeboats would only clutter up the decks and, after all, *Titanic* was unsinkable.

On that fateful night in April 1912, after *Titanic* struck the iceberg in the middle of the North Atlantic, chaos broke out on board when it became apparent that there were not enough lifeboats to accommodate all of the passengers and crew. In the midst of that chaos, Bruce Ismay, who was on *Titanic's* maiden voyage, stepped into a lifeboat that was not full and was winched to safety. Witnesses say that he sat staring at the horizon ahead of him, his back to the sight of *Titanic* breaking in half and sinking beneath the icy waves. Once on board the *Carpathia* he was sedated and it is said that his hair turned white overnight.

In the wake of the disaster, Ismay became the most hated person in America and Britain. He had left his own ship to sink to a watery grave along with over 1,500 souls. He was dubbed the 'Coward of the *Titanic*'. He resigned from The White Star Line, and testified at the inquiry that he had left an empty ship.

After the inquiry, Ismay and his wife moved to Costello Lodge in Connemara, where he lived a quiet life out of the public eye. He never spoke about the *Titanic*. He remained in Connemara for twenty-five years, only leaving when his health failed. He died in London in 1937 from complications due to diabetes.

Another link between Galway and *Titanic* is John George 'Jack' Phillips, the senior wireless operator on board. From Goldalming in England, he was employed by the Marconi Telegraphy Company and worked on ships such as White Star's *Teutonic* and Cunard's *Lusitania* as a junior wireless operator. In 1908 he was sent to work at the Marconi Station near Clifden, where he spent three years, before returning to sea. In 1912 Jack was sent to Belfast to install the wireless telegraph equipment on *Titanic* and was given the job of senior wireless operator on the maiden voyage. It was Jack Phillips who sent out the distress signals and continued to do so until the power on board failed. He did not survive the disaster.

The SS Athenia

The SS *Athenia* was a passenger ship which sailed between Britain and Canada in the 1930s. On 2 September 1939 she left Glasgow, stopped at Liverpool and Belfast to take on more passengers before she made her way around the north coast of Ireland and out into the Atlantic.

At 11 a.m. on Sunday 3 September 1939, Britain declared war on Germany. The *Athenia* was about 250 miles off the Irish coast when, a few hours after the declaration, she was torpedoed by a German U-boat. She was the first casualty of the Second World War. There were 1,103 passengers and 315 crew on board.

A Norwegian tanker, the *Knute Nelson*, and a number of British naval vessels hurried to the scene to assist the sinking ship. One hundred and seventeen people lost their lives. The captain of the *Knute Nelson* was ordered to take 430 survivors to the nearest neutral port. He headed for Galway. He radioed ahead and the harbourmaster alerted the authorities. By the time the tanker reached Galway Bay, everyone who could be mobilised to help was ready. Even the Girl Guides had been drafted in to help.

A tender boat carrying doctors, nurses and members of the Gardaí and army were the first to meet the survivors, bringing back the most seriously wounded, who were taken to hospital. The walking wounded were then brought ashore and given clothing, food and accommodation in the city. After a few days the passengers were sent by train to Dublin, from where some of them continued to Belfast while others crossed back to Britain, all of them grateful for the hospitality they had received in Galway.

Dutch KLM Super Constellation Crash

On 14 August 1958, a KLM Royal Dutch Airlines Super Constellation aeroplane was en route from Amsterdam to New York, via Shannon. The *Hugo De Groot* had left Shannon and was 100 miles off the coast of Connemara when it crashed into the Atlantic Ocean. Boats, including the Aran Islands Ferry boat, the *Naomh Éanna*, headed to the scene of the disaster, but tragically all eight crew members and ninety-one passengers were killed. The dead were brought to Galway by various fishing trawlers and a Canadian naval ship. Only thirty-four bodies were recovered and twenty-two were never properly identified. Many were buried in the new cemetery, Bohermore.

Alcock and Brown

What could have been a disaster turned into a record-breaking achievement for two aviators in 1919. In June of that year, sixteen years after the Wright Brothers had successfully made their first flight at Kittyhawk, two intrepid aviators, Captain John Alcock and his navigator Lieutenant Arthur Whitten Brown, took to the air in a Vickers Vimy biplane, intent on crossing the Atlantic Ocean. Their aim was to win the £10,000 prize being offered by the *Daily Mail* newspaper to the pilots who managed the first non-stop flight between North America and Europe.

Both men had grown up in Manchester and were experienced pilots, having served in the Royal Flying Corps during the First World War. They left from St John's in Newfoundland, and after sixteen hours and 1,900 miles, they saw the Irish coastline come into view. They needed a flat, firm piece of ground to land their plane. They saw what looked like a suitable place near the town of Clifden. It might have looked suitable, but the Derrygimlagh Bog where Alcock and Brown landed on 15 June 1919 was far from flat or firm. Fortunately, only the plane was damaged in the bumpy landing. Word of their success was sent to London from the nearby Marconi Station. Alcock and Brown were given knighthoods and later collected the prize money, which was presented to them by Winston Churchill. Sadly Alcock died in a flying accident later that same year. Arthur Brown died in 1948.

There are two monuments in the Clifden area commemorating the remarkable achievement of Alcock and Brown. The first is a white cairn located near the actual landing site in the bog. The other is a sculpture of an aeroplane's tailfin, which was erected to commemorate the fortieth anniversary of the landing. It is on a hill overlooking the Derrygimlagh Bog.

8

BITS AND PIECES

SPECIAL VISITS TO GALWAY

Royal Visits
King Edward VII and Queen Alexandra made a state visit to Ireland in 1903 and included Galway in their itinerary. They arrived on the royal yacht, the *Victoria and Albert*, which docked at Killary Harbour. There the royal couple and their party were transferred to a fleet of cars, at a time when cars were a rare sight on the roads of Connemara. They were brought via Letterfrack to Kylemore Castle, as it was then known, for tea. It is thought that the king considered buying Kylemore, but it was too remote and would have been too costly for him to maintain. The royal couple had lunch at Recess and then boarded the train for their journey to Galway city.

King Edward's great great grandson, Prince Charles and his wife, the Duchess of Cornwall visited Galway in 2015 and stayed at the Lough Cutra Estate outside Gort.

President John Fitzgerald Kennedy
The thirty-fifth President of the United States of America, John Fitzgerald Kennedy, visited Ireland in June 1963. His family was originally from New Ross in Co. Wexford. During a packed four-day visit, he made time to visit the city of Galway. He arrived by helicopter on a dull day and landed in the Galway Sportsground, where he was greeted by the Mayor of Galway Patrick D. Ryan.

Children from the nearby Mercy School dressed in rain capes of green, white, orange and brown were arranged into an Irish tricolour with a brown flagpole. Before leaving the Sportsground for the cavalcade which would take him to Eyre Square, President Kennedy made an unscheduled stop to talk to the children, who gave him an impromptu rendition of 'Galway Bay'.

In Eyre Square 100,000 Galwegians had gathered to hear the American president make a speech on the contribution of Irish immigrants to America. He was made a Freeman of the City, before the cavalcade continued through the streets to Salthill, where the president's helicopter waited to whisk him on to his next engagement.

The president was killed in Dallas five months later, in November 1963.

The Papal Visit of 1979

One of the biggest gatherings ever seen in Galway was the crowd of 200,000 people who assembled at Ballybrit Racecourse on the east of Galway city on Sunday, 30 September 1979 to hear Pope John Paul II say mass for the Youth of Ireland.

The newly created Pope was on his second international trip and was spending three days in Ireland, being whisked from city to city by helicopter. From the early hours on Sunday morning, crowds from all over the county and busloads of teenagers representing Youth clubs from all over Ireland began streaming into the racecourse. Fr Michael Cleary of Dublin and Bishop Eamon Casey, then Bishop of Galway, were the 'warm-up act' on what was a cold, misty morning. At 10.30 a.m. the rotors of the helicopter bringing the Pope from his previous engagement at Clonmacnoise could be heard approaching and soon appeared out of the misty sky, a figure dressed in white waving from the window to the assembled congregation below.

The most poignant moment of the day came during the Pope's homily, when he declared, 'Young people of Ireland, I love you'. It was a momentous day not just for Galway, but for the youth of the country.

Four thousand volunteers helped the emergency services to marshal the huge crowd. Over the course of that day, 1,000 people were treated by doctors, and thirty-six needed to be hospitalised, including two heart attacks and one fatality.

The Gardaí had to deal mainly with crowd management, traffic control and lost teenagers!

UNIQUE HERITAGE OF GALWAY

Galway Hookers and Currachs

The Galway hooker, a traditional sail boat, was once the workhorse of Galway Bay. Over the centuries, Galway seafarers have used the hooker for fishing and transport. The origins of this traditional boat, which is only found in this part of Ireland, are uncertain. Similar boats can be found from Scandinavia to North Africa, but the name suggests that perhaps it originated from the traditional Dutch *hoeker* fishing boat. From the sixteenth century, the Dutch used the *hoeker* to fish for cod in the North Sea, off the Hook of Holland. By the eighteenth century the *hoeker* was used for trading goods with England and maybe even as far away as Galway.

As they were originally used for fishing, it is also possible that the name of the boat came from the hook and line method of fishing that was used in Galway Bay for centuries.

The Galway hooker is built from oak. There are four different sizes. 'An Bád Mór', as the Irish name suggests, is the 'big boat' and at 13m (44ft) is the largest of the hookers. The other three are the *leathbhád*, or 'half boat', the *gleotoig* and the *púcán*, which is the smallest at 7m (20ft). The Galway hooker is wide and curved at the middle, and has a mast at the centre from

GALWAY 'HOOKER'

which are unfurled a main sail and two foresails. The sails are either reddish brown or black in colour. This colour comes from the tree bark solution which is applied to the calico sails each year to make them waterproof.

By the 1730s, the 'Tribes of Galway' had fallen out of favour. The full force of the Penal Laws prevented them from carrying on their traditional trade. Some of the families turned to smuggling. With so many boats, and in particular Galway hookers, coming into Galway docks carrying turf, wood and passengers from Connemara, it would have been impossible for the authorities to check every cargo.

One noteworthy smuggling escapade occurred in 1735. James Brown and Martin Blake, both descendants of the Tribes, agreed to collaborate in a venture to buy local wool and smuggle it to Nantes in France. At that time wool from Ireland could only be sold in England. They loaded the wool onto Galway hookers at Oranmore and moved it through Galway Bay to Roundstone under the nose of a British naval man-of-war, the *Spy*, which was docked in the bay. At Roundstone the cargo was transferred to a ship Brown and Blake had hired from Cork for the voyage to France. They planned to return to Galway with a cargo of brandy and tea, goods which had to come into Ireland via England. However, Bryan McDonogh, who had been employed by Brown and Blake to help with the enterprise, alerted the authorities to the caper after he fell out with them. Brown was arrested and sent to Fleet Prison in London. McDonogh was then kidnapped by the Blakes, but was eventually released.

Because the Galway coastline alternates between beaches and rugged rocky seashore, the Galway hookers could not make land easily. In the absence of built harbours and piers, the services of another traditional Galway boat were needed to bring cargos from the hooker safely to shore. The currach is a wooden-framed rowing boat with no keel. Originally the frame was covered with animal hides, but by the eighteenth century it was covered with canvas and then coated with tar to make it watertight. The currach is propelled by wooden oars, rowed by between one and four oarsmen. As the hookers docked in the bays and inlets, their cargos were loaded into currachs and brought safely to the beaches.

From the mid-1800s, roads and railways made the interior of Connemara more accessible to and from Galway, reducing dependency on the sea for transport. By the 1970s just two working hookers remained in use. Today there are preservation programmes in place to ensure that the craft of building these traditional boats is kept alive. The Galway Hooker Association was founded in 1978 to maintain the two boats, but also to build new ones and to ensure that the Galway coast would always have hookers. They organised regattas and gatherings. The first Crinniú na mBád Festival was held in Kinvara in 1979.

Aran Jumpers, the Críos and Pampooties

When the Irish folk group the Clancy Brothers and Tommy Makem began wearing Aran jumpers for their stage performances in the 1950s, this uniquely Irish garment which has its humble origins on the remote Co. Galway islands suddenly became a fashion item. Traditionally the jumpers were made from a wool known in Irish as *báinín*. Because the wool was not stripped of its natural oils, and remained water repellent,

it was the ideal material from which to make clothing for fishermen. The women of the Aran Islands knitted the yarn into jumpers, using intricate combinations of cable stitches which resulted in a thick, durable garment. It is said that women knitted the same pattern for the men folk in their family. The consistent patterns served a practical purpose. In the event of a fishing tragedy, and there were many, when the corpse of a fisherman was washed ashore, his jumper allowed the islanders to identify which family he came from. He could then be buried in the appropriate family plot.

Another item of clothing particular to the Aran Islands was the *crios*. *Crios* is the Irish word for belt. The women of the islands hand-wove a colourful narrow woollen strip, fringed at either end, which was worn around the waist. It served only a decorative purpose.

The Aran islanders also had their own unique footwear, known as pampooties. These were made from rawhide, often with the hairs of the animal still attached. A single piece of untanned leather was wrapped around the foot, and stitched in place with twine. The shoes were soft and water resistant and, like the Aran jumpers, ideal for the fishermen of the islands. Pampooties also had a practical purpose. The fishermen needed to wear soft shoes so that they did not puncture the light canvas covering of the the traditional currach boats. Today the soft Irish dancing shoes bear a similarity to the pampooties.

GALWAY AND HORSES

Fox hunting

In the past, fox hunting was the pursuit of the landed gentry. Their winter months were filled with the thrill of the chase, made all the more thrilling in parts of Galway as the horses faced a challenging terrain lined with stone walls. In 1803 Burton Persse of Moyode Castle near Athenry, who had the best pack of foxhounds in the county, made a gift of his best animals to his nephew, Robert Parson Persse. He lived at Castleboy near Kilchreest, where he formed the Castleboy Hunt, which later became the County Galway Hunt. In the early days of the Castleboy Hunt they had a standing invitation to attend a meet with Colonel Eyre's hunt at Eyrecourt. After one exhilarating meet, the huntsmen retreated to Dooley's Hotel in Birr. The revelries got out of hand and the hotel was set on fire, earning the Castleboy Hunt the nickname 'the Galway Blazers'.

The film director John Huston was Joint Master of the Foxhounds with the Galway Blazers during the 1960s, and the hunt gathered at his home, St Clerans, for the St Stephen's Day meet during this time. Today the Galway Blazers still hunt in the area of Craughwell, meeting three days a week between October and March.

The Galway Races

One of Galway's most famous festivals is the Galway Races. The 4th Earl of Howth, Lord William Ulick Tristram St Lawrence, MP for the Borough of Galway and a member of the County Galway Hunt, is credited as the founder of the Galway Races. In 1869 he moved a race meeting that usually took place in Loughrea to Ballybrit on the edge of Galway city. The first meeting of the Galway Races was held on 17 August that year. The first day of the two-day event was attended by 40,000 people. Four races were run on the 1.5-mile track at Ballybrit. The biggest prize was the Galway Plate, worth 100 sovereigns (£105). The Galway Plate has been run every year since, except in 1922 when races were cancelled due to the hostilities of the Civil War. Today the Galway Races is a seven-day festival. In 2015, 140,000 people attended.

Ballinasloe Horse Fair

During the nineteenth century, hundreds of horse fairs were held around Ireland. People came to trade horses but also to trade news. For many it was the main social event of the year. In Co. Galway a number of horse fairs have endured into the twenty-first century, the Ballinasloe Fair and the Maam Cross Fair being the two most notable.

The Irish name for Ballinasloe is 'Beal-Atha-na-Sluaigheadh', which translates as 'the ford mouth of the gatherings'. It is where east meets west, where Connacht meets Leinster. In the seventeenth century Ballinasloe hosted fairs for the sale of cattle and sheep. Animals fattened on the rich pasture land of the Midlands were brought west, sold to merchants who slaughtered them, salted the meat and sold it to the British West India fleet which came into Galway port. This trade continued until the 1790s. Later, the traffic went in the other direction, with farmers in Connacht breeding cattle and selling them to Midland farmers for fattening.

Originally there were three Ballinasloe fairs, held in May, July and October. At the July fair, which often lasted six weeks, wool was traded. The other two fairs were mainly for the sale of livestock. In 1801, an article in the *London Times* referred to the 'great cattle fair of Ballinasloe' and in 1835 a visitor to the October fair recorded the sale of 55,000 sheep and 7,000 cattle.

By the late eighteenth century horses were also being traded at Balliansloe. Quartermasters from European armies, who had a high regard for the calibre of Irish horses on offer, came to buy horses for their cavalries. It is thought that Napoleon's favourite horse, Marengo, named after the Battle of Marengo in 1800, was bought at the Ballinasloe Horse Fair.

The extension of the Grand Canal to Ballinasloe in 1828 linked the town with Dublin, and led to an increase in trade. When the railways arrived some decades later, the movement of livestock became more efficient. By the late nineteenth century, the wool trade had been significantly reduced and by the twentieth century marts around the country took over the trade in cattle. All that was left to trade at Ballinasloe was horses.

By the 1940s the horse fair too was under threat of dying out as mechanised vehicles meant that demand for horses was dwindling. A committee was set up and a carnival was added to the fair to create a festival atmosphere. In addition to being a horse fair, the event became a horse show, with competitions for best horse and best pony. Today the fair also has a dog show. An estimated 80,000 attended the 2015 event with buyers coming from Great Britain and continental Europe to buy Irish horses.

SPORT IN GALWAY

The Gaelic Athletic Association
One of Ireland's most enduring and influential institutions is the Gaelic Athletic Association (GAA). Founded in 1884, it was the brainchild of Michael Cusack (1847–1906), who wanted to revive the ancient Irish game of hurling and the game of Gaelic football. The story of the GAA began, not in Thurles as is often recorded, but in Co. Galway.

Cusack was from Co. Clare. He was a teacher and taught at Lough Cutra National School between 1867 and 1871. He then moved to Dublin, where he founded the Metropolitan Hurling Club. At that time, the game was played throughout Ireland but there were no formal competitions. At Easter of 1884, the Metropolitan Hurling Club was invited to Co. Galway to play a challenge match against a team from the village of Killimor in East Galway. The game was played on the Fair Green in Ballinasloe that Easter Monday. The chaos that Michael Cusack witnessed on the pitch that day impressed upon him the need for a standardised set of rules. A governing body for the sport was needed.

That August Cusack was back in Co. Galway where at a meeting with like-minded people in Loughrea, he outlined his idea for an association that would regulate Gaelic games. He had hoped to enlist the help of Bishop Duggan of Clonfert, who had been a hurler in his youth. The aging bishop declined, citing ill health, but suggested that if Cusack wanted the patronage of a bishop, he should contact Archbishop Croke of Cashel and Emly. It was this suggestion that led Michael Cusack to set up the meeting at Hayes's Hotel in Thurles, Co. Tipperary on 1 November 1884, where the Gaelic Athletic Association was founded.

All-Ireland Senior Football Championship

Galway has won the All-Ireland Senior Football Championship and brought the Sam Maguire Cup across the Shannon nine times since the first championship final was played in 1887. The proudest of these wins was in 1966, as the Cup was making its third consecutive trip to Galway, for the famous 'Three in a Row':

1964	Galway	0–15 (15 points)	Kerry	0–10 (10 points)
1965	Galway	0–12 (12 points)	Kerry	0–09 (9 points)
1966	Galway	1–10 (13 points)	Meath	0–07 (7 points)

The other victories were in 1925, 1934, 1938, 1956, 1998 and 2001.

All-Ireland Senior Hurling Championship
Galway played in the first ever All-Ireland Hurling Final in 1887, but did not bring home the title. In twenty-one finals, Galway has won the Liam McCarthy Cup on five occasions, three of these during the 1980s and most recently in 2017:

1923	Galway	7–3 (24 points)	Limerick	4–5 (17 points)
1980	Galway	2–15 (21 points)	Limerick	3–9 (18 points)
1987	Galway	1–12 (15 points)	Kilkenny	0–9 (9 points)
1988	Galway	1–15 (18 points)	Tipperary	0–14 (14 points)
2017	Galway	0–26 (26 points)	Waterford	2–17 (23 points)

All-Ireland Senior Camogie Final
In the ladies' hurling, Galway has won the O'Duffy Cup twice, out of seventeen finals since the first in 1932:

| 1996 | Galway | 4–8 (20 points) | Cork | 1–15 (18 points) |
| 2013 | Galway | 1–9 (12 points) | Kilkenny | 0–7 (7 points) |

All-Ireland Senior Ladies' Football Final
Since it was first played in 1974, Galway has appeared in three finals and brought the Brendan Martin Cup home once:

| 2004 | Galway | 3–8 (17 points) | Dublin | 0–11 (11 points) |

Galway Olympians
The first Galway man to compete in an Olympic Games was Cummin Clancy of Oughterard, who competed in the discus in the London Games of 1948.

Francis Barrett from Galway was the flag-bearer for the Irish team at the 1996 Atlanta Games. He competed as a light middle-weight boxer.

Olive Loughnane grew up in the village of Carrabane, near Loughrea. She competed in the 20km walk event at four Olympic Games between 2000 and 2012. In 2009 she won a silver medal at the World Championships held in Berlin. In 2016 she was awarded the gold medal in that event, as the original gold medallist, Russian Olga Kaniskina, was disqualified for doping.

Paul Hession is a sprinter from Galway. He competed in the Beijing Games in 2008, making it to the semi-final of the 200m. He finished fifth, just out of contention for a place in the final. He also competed at the London Games in 2012.

Oarsman Cormac Folan of Barna competed in the Coxless Four event at the Beijing Games in 2008.

Galway Golfing Greats

Galway can boast two golfing greats. Christy O'Connor Senior (1924–2016), better known in the golfing fraternity as 'Himself', was born at Knocknacarra, Salthill almost within sight of Galway Golf Club. The members of Tuam Golf Club raised the £70 entrance fee he needed to enter his first professional tournament, the 1951 Open played at Portrush. He won the Irish Pro-Am ten times and between 1955 and 1973 played in ten consecutive Ryder Cups. Gifted with a natural swing, he won twenty-four titles on the European Tour, including the British Masters in 1955 and 1959.

The other great golfer to come from Galway was Christy O'Connor Senior's nephew, Christy O'Connor Junior (1948–2016). Like his uncle, he was born in Knocknacarra. After turning professional in 1967, he had seventeen professional wins, including the British Masters in 1992, and two Ryder Cup appearances in 1975 and 1989. In later years he turned his hand to course design.

Rugby in Galway

The Connacht rugby team was founded in 1885 to field a team for the interprovincial championship with Leinster, Munster and Ulster. In the amateur era, the teams only played three matches in the year. Since the advent of the professional era, the provincial teams have more competitions. Connacht's biggest achievement came in 2016 when they beat Leinster in the Guinness Pro12 Final, their first major trophy in their 121-year history.

A number of Connacht players have been capped for Ireland. The first Connacht player to win an Irish cap was George Henebrey, who won six between 1906 and 1909.

Ciaran Fitzgerald was born in Loughrea in 1952. He captained Ireland to two Triple Crown wins in 1982 and 1985 and a Five Nations Championship win in 1983. He captained the British and Irish Lions Team that toured New Zealand in 1983.

Eric Elwood was born in Galway in 1969 and played for Ireland between 1995 and 2002, scoring 296 points.

Jerry Flannery was born in Galway. He played for Connacht, but is better known for playing as hooker for Munster between 2003 and 2012, during which time Munster won the Heineken Cup in 2006 and 2008. He won forty-one caps playing for Ireland and was on the Grand Slam winning team of 2009.

Noel Mannion played for Connacht and Ireland, making sixteen appearances in the green jersey between 1988 and 1993.

Soccer in Galway
Galway Rovers Football Club was set up in the Claddagh area of Galway in 1937. The club joined the Football Association of Ireland (FAI) League of Ireland in 1977 and changed its name to Galway United, playing their home games at Terryland. They won the FAI Cup in 1991.

OTHER BITS AND PIECES

Connaught or Connacht?
Celtic Ireland was divided into the four kingdoms of Ulster in the north, Leinster in the east, Munster in the south and Connacht in the west. The only purpose these regions serve today is to provide Ireland with professional rugby teams.

Connacht is traditionally made up of Galway, Mayo, Sligo, Roscommona and Leitrim. The Irish spelling is 'Connacht'. The alternative spelling of 'Connaught' is the anglicised version. The Connacht Tribune and the Connacht rugby team use the Irish spelling while the now-disbanded Connaught Rangers used the English form. When Queen Victoria decided to give her son

Arthur a dukedom, he was created Duke of Connaught. London's Connaught Hotel was called after him. The title is now extinct.

The Orient Express

In the 1990s two carriages from the Orient Express train made their way to Galway and were placed outside the Glenlo Abbey Hotel. The carriages date from 1927 and in their heyday were used on the Orient Express train route from Paris to Istanbul and St Petersburg. One of the carriages was used in the 1974 film version of Agatha Christie's *Murder on the Orient Express*. Today the two carriages are used as a restaurant by the hotel.

The MV Plassy

In the opening credits of the popular 1990s television comedy series *Father Ted*, a shipwreck is seen perched on a beach on the edge of an island. This is the wreck of the freight ship MV *Plassey*. In March 1960 she was travelling from Fenit in Co. Kerry to Galway with a general cargo when a she got caught in a storm. The ship was washed ashore on Inishsheer. The islanders rescued the eleven crew members using a breeches buoy. When the storm abated the locals helped themselves to some of the cargo of Scotch whisky, biscuits and wool. The wreck has been shifted further inland by various storms in the years since the ship was washed ashore.

George Washington

Colonel William Persse (*c*. 1728–1802) fought in the American War of Independence. He became friendly with George Washington, with whom he shared an interest in horticulture. On returning to Ireland and the family estate at Roxborough, between Gort and Loughrea, William sent Washington some gooseberry bushes.

He was the great-grandfather of Lady Augusta Gregory.

Sir Hudson Lowe, Napoleon's Gaoler (1769–1844)

Sir Hudson Lowe has a very tentative link to Galway. His mother was a Morgan from Galway city, and he was born there in 1769. His family left Galway for the West Indies a year later, never to return.

He is most famous for serving as the governor of the island of St Helena from 1816 to 1821, during the years when Napoleon

Bonaparte was kept captive there after his defeat at the Battle of Waterloo in 1815. There were several connections in the lives of Lowe and Napoleon. They were the same age, Lowe had spent time at Ajaccio in Corsica (where Napoleon was born), and was given the task of delivering the news of Napoleon's first abdication to London in 1814.

While on St Helena the two soldiers only met six times and conversed in Italian. The meetings did not go well. The surgeon appointed as Napoleon's physician, Irishman Barry Edward O'Meara, felt that Lowe had mistreated Napoleon and when he wrote this in his memoirs Lowe instigated a defamation lawsuit, but it never came to the courts.

Also on St Helena at that time was Major Poppleton, who was charged with supervising the captive Napoleon at Longwood House. Unlike Lowe, Poppleton did get on with Napoleon and when he was asked to spy on his charge, he refused and resigned. Before leaving St Helena, it is said that Napoleon gave him a snuffbox. Poppleton left the army and returned to his wife's home, Ross Castle in Co. Galway.

A Modern Irish Brand

Supermac's, the fast-food restaurant, that most Irish of Irish brands, has its origins in Co. Galway. The first ever Supermac's was opened on Main Street, Ballinasloe in 1978, serving burgers and chips to the town's late-night revellers. Today there are 160 outlets throughout the country.

Lunch atop a Skyscraper

In 1932 an unknown photographer took a photograph of a group of eleven workmen as they had their lunch. The photograph has become iconic, as the workers are seen sitting on a girder suspended 800ft above New York, with no safety harnesses or helmets. In recent years it has been suggested that two of the figures were originally from Shaneaglish in Galway, possibly Matty O'Shaughnessy and Sonny Glynn, who emigrated to America in the 1920s.

BIBLIOGRAPHY

BOOKS

Burke, Ray, *Joyce County: Galway and Joyce* (Dublin: Currach Press, 2016).

Claffey, Dr J.A., *A Brief History of Tuam: A Town of Two Cathedrals* (Galway, 2006).

Connolly, S.J., *The Oxford Companion to Irish History* (Oxford: Oxford University Press, 1998).

Conwell, John Joseph, *A Galway Landlord during the Great Famine: Ulick John de Burgh, First Marquis of Clanricarde* (Dublin: Four Courts Press, 2003).

De Búrca, Marcus, *The GAA: A History* (Dublin: Gill and MacMillan, 2000).

Duffy, Sean (ed.), *Atlas of Irish History* (Dublin: Gill and Macmillan, 2000).

Fahy, Mary de Lourdes, *Kiltartan: Many Leaves One Root A History of the Parish of Kiltartan* (Gort: Kiltartan Gregory Cultural Society, 2004.

Feehan, J. and G. O'Donovan, *The Magic of Coole Park* (Dublin: OPW, 1993).

Halpin, Andy and Conor Newman, *Ireland: An Oxford Archaeological Guide* (Oxford: Oxford University Press, 2006).

Hanley, Mary and Liam Miller, *Thoor Ballylee, Home of William Butler Yeats* (Dublin: Dolmen Press, 1977).

Harbison, Peter, *A Thousand Years of Church Heritage in East Galway* (Dublin: Ashfield Press, 2005).

Healy, Ann, *Athenry: A Brief History and Guide* (A. Healy, 1988).

Hegarty, Shane and Fintan O'Toole, *The Irish Times Book of the 1916 Rising* (Dublin: Gill and MacMillan, 2006).

Henry, William, *Famine: Galway's Darkest Years* (Cork: Mercier Press, 2011).

Henry, William, *St Clerans: The Tale of a Manor House* (Galway: Merv Griffin, 1999).

Humphreys, Madeleine, *The Life and Times of Edward Martyn: An Aristocratic Bohemian* (Dublin: Irish Academic Press, 2007).

Kee, Robert, *Ireland: A History* (London: Abacus, 1995).

Kelly, Declan, *Loughrea: A Parish History* (Dublin: The History Press Ireland, 2014).

Kohfeldt, Mary Lou, *Lady Gregory: The Woman behind the Irish Renaissance* (London: Andre Deutsch Ltd, 1985).

Lysaght, Charles (ed.), *Great Irish Lives* (London: HarperCollins, 2008).

MacMahon, M., *Portumna Castle and its Lords* (Portumna, 2000).

Madden, Gerard, *Sliabh Aughty Ramble* (Tuamgraney: East Clare Heritage, 2010).

Monahan, Phelim O.D.C., *The Old Abbey Loughrea, 1300–1650* (Loughrea: P. Monahan, 1982).

Mosely, Charlotte (ed.), *The Mitfords: Letters between Six Sisters* (London: Harper Perennial, 2007).

Mulvihill, Mary, *Ingenious Ireland: A County-by-County Exploration of Irish Mysteries and Marvels* (Dublin: TownHouse and CountryHouse Ltd, 2002).

O'Brien, Jacqueline, and Peter Harbison, *Ancient Ireland from Prehistory to the Middle Ages* (London: Weidenfeld & Nicholson, 1996).

O'Byrne, Robert, *Hugh Lane, 1875–1915* (Dublin: The Lilliput Press Ltd, 2000).

O'Connor, Kevin, *Ironing the Land: Coming of the Railways to Ireland* (Dublin: Gill and MacMillan, 1999).

O'Connor, Ulick, *Celtic Dawn: A Portrait of Irish Renaissance* (Dublin: TownHouse and CountryHouse, 1999).

O'Connor, Ulick, *The Troubles* (London: Mandarin Paperbacks, 1996).

O'Dowd, Peadar, *Old and New Galway* (Galway: The Archaeological Historical and Folklore Society RTC Galway and The Connacht Tribune Ltd, 1985).

Ó'Laoi, Pádraic, *Fr. Griffin, 1892–1920* (Printed by The Connacht Tribune, 1994).

O'Rourke, Con, *Nature Guide to the Aran Islands* (Dublin: The Lilliput Press, 2006).

Robinson, Tim, *Connemara: The Last Pool of Darkness* (Dublin: Penguin Ireland, 2008).

Scott Wheeler, James, *Cromwell in Ireland* (Dublin: Gill and Macmillan, 1999).

Spellissy, Sean, *The History of Galway, City and County* (Limerick: The Celtic Bookshop, 1999).

Walsh, Paul, *Discover Galway* (Dublin: The O'Brien Press Ltd, 2001).

JOURNALS AND MAGAZINES

Carroll, Francis M., '"The First Casualty of the Sea": The *Athenia* Survivors and the Galway Relief Effort, September 1939', *History Ireland*, vol. 19, no. 1 (January–February 2011), 42–45.

Collins, Timothy, 'From Hoekers to Hookers: A Survey of the Literature and Annotated Bibliography on the Origins of the Galway Hooker', *Journal of The Galway Archaeological and Historical Society*, vol. 53 (2001), 66–83.

Cronin, John, '"A Gentleman of Good Family and Fortune": John Eyre of Eyrecourt (1640–1685)', *Journal of The Galway Archaeological and Historical Society*, vol. 60 (2006), 88–125.

Cullen, Louis M., 'Five Letters Relating to Galway Smuggling in 1737', *Journal of The Galway Archaeological and Historical Society*, vol. 27 (1956–1957), 10–25.

Cullen, Louis M., 'The Galway Smuggling Trade in the Seventeen-Thirties', *Journal of The Galway Archaeological and Historical Society*, vol. 30, no. 1–2 (1962–1963), 7–40.

Geddes, Goerge, 'The Buildings of the Loughrea to Attymon Light Railway', *Journal of The Galway Archaeological and Historical Society*, vol. 59 (2007), 168–178.

Hoare, Kieran, 'A Guide to the Archival Holdings of the James Hardiman Library, NUI, Galway', *Journal of The Galway Archaeological and Historical Society*, vol. 53 (2001), 84–104.

Kennedy, Patrick, 'The County of the Town of Galway', *Journal of The Galway Archaeological and Historical Society*, vol. 30, no. 3–4 (1962–1963), 90–102.

Mannion, Joseph, 'Vestiges of Celtic Mythology in the place names of Lough Corrib and its Hinterlands', *Journal of The Galway Archaeological and Historical Society*, vol. 59 (2007), 18–24.

Mercer, Bríd, '"A Seat Improved Entirely in the Modern English Taste": The History of Woodlawn Estate, 1550–1800', *Journal of The Galway Archaeological and Historical Society*, vol. 63 (2011), 73–87.

Mohr, Paul, 'The De Berminghams Barons of Athenry: A Suggested Outline Lineage, from First to Last', *Journal of The Galway Archaeological and Historical Society*, vol. 63 (2011), 43–56.

Mullane, Fidelma, 'Distorted Views of the People and their Houses in the Claddagh in the Nineteenth Century', *Journal of The Galway Archaeological and Historical Society*, vol. 61 (2009), 170–200.

Stratton Ryan, Mary, '*A Dynamic Irishman in Paris*: Patrick d'Arcy 1725–79', *History Ireland*, vol. 18, no. 2 (March–April 2010), 22–23.

Walsh Anne, 'Galway Landlords and Country Houses', *Journal of The Galway Archaeological and Historical Society*, vol. 42 (1989–1990), 114–124.

WEBSITES

www.galway.ie
www.historyireland.ie
www.advertiser.ie
www.irishtimes.com
www.imdb.com

ABOUT THE AUTHOR

HELEN LEE has been a tour guide since 1994, working across Ireland and Britain. In 2004 she was awarded her Galway Tour Guide Badge by Fáilte Ireland and now regularly conducts walking tours of Galway City.

I would like to thank family, friends and colleagues who have been supportive throughout the writing of this book. I would particularly like to thank Anne Dunne, Barbara McCarthy and Liz Ryan who read drafts of chapters.